The Prophet to the Nation:
America
Under Judgment

RODERICK AGUILLARD

Copyright © 2011 by Roderick Aguillard

All rights reserved. No part of this book may be used, reproduced, stored in a retrieval system, or transmitted in any form whatsoever — including electronic, photocopy, recording — without prior written permission from the author, except in the case of brief quotations embodied in critical articles or reviews.

All scripture quotations, unless otherwise indicated, are taken from the Holy Bible, King James Version. KJV. Public Domain.

FIRST EDITION

ISBN: 9781936989379

Library of Congress Control Number: 2011945641

Published by
NewBookPublishing.com, a division of Reliance Media, Inc.
2395 Apopka Blvd., #200, Apopka, FL 32703
NewBookPublishing.com

Printed in the United States of America

Table of Contents

Author's Gratitude 5

Foreword 7

Chapter 1: God's Callings And Commission 9

Chapter 2: The Apostle And The Prophet To The Body 17

Chapter 3: The Prophet: The Seer To The Nation 27

Chapter 4: The Redemptive Nature Of God's Judgment 41

Chapter 5: The Prophets Warning:
God Is At War With Evil 51

Chapter 6: Apostolic Fathers: Prophetic Sons And
Daughters (The Elisha Generation) 69

Chapter 7: The Prophet To The Nation:
Three Stages Of God's Judgments On A Nation 79

Chapter 8: The Seven Sealed Book And
The Season Of The Seals 103

Chapter 9: Israel And The Final Wars
Of The Middle East 119

Chapter 10: The Seventieth Week:
The Day Of The Lord, The Final Seven Years 133

Chapter 11: God's Last Call For Intercessors 147

2-19-12

To Dave & Lynda,
   Great to know
you & yours!
Let's go fishing!

    Red Mullett

Author's Gratitude:

First of all I am very grateful for my wife of fifty-two years, Marvelous Mary, who has been my chief cheerleader. She has encouraged me throughout my ministry. "Her husband is known in the gates, when he sits among the elders of the land." Proverbs 31:23. I am her husband and I am honored among the elders because she completes me. Secondly, Pam Kirkwood my executive assistant has been diligent in typing my manuscript for this book. She spent days and weeks working to put this book together for printing. Mary and I love her dearly and deeply appreciate her service to our ministry.

Rod Aguillard

Foreword

It's not very often I am called upon to write a foreword for someone I can truly say I have walked together with. For over 30 years, my life has been intertwined with Rod and Mary Aguillard's and all of it has been positive, fun, and powerful.

Rod Aguillard carries the mantle of a prophet. In our world of "pastor/teacher" heroes, Rod's gift is pursued by some and shunned by others. Any prophet is usually "without honor in his own country." However, I am totally convinced that the evangelistic, prophetic, and apostolic are just as needed today as they were 2000 years ago when Paul listed them in Ephesians 4: 11.

The prophet is a "seer." No wonder Rod is so keenly interested in and qualified to look at the Revelation of John in application to today's rapidly changing world events. A "seer" sees behind the scenes. He *perceives* the mind of God as it is not apparent to others. He moves greatly in the revelation and vocal gifts of the Spirit. He has a vision for a nation, and in Rod's case it is America.

Rod's heart for America was first apparent in his national leadership of the pro-life movement. For many months, he was consumed with bringing this issue to the conscience of a nation. He has also been consumed with revival and restoration. His messages are fiery, powerful, and unforgettable. He lives the fire of revival twenty-four hours a day.

Now, his great passion is the end of time. What would Daniel give to be sitting where we sit today? Where are the prophets like Daniel who can tell us what is the word of the Lord? Perhaps you are holding one of those voices in your hand. Read this book with an open mind and heart. NO ONE knows the day or the hour. NO ONE can harshly predict the exact workings of the Revelation as it comes to pass. However, the spirit of those warnings and blessings and events can be on our mind continually as we look to the skies to welcome our Lord and Savior Jesus Christ.

I'm sure you will find something in this book to take issue with. My father always said, "Eat the meat and spit out the bones!" However, I can testify of the impeccable character and integrity of the author. A servant, a teacher, a father, an encourager, and one of my lifetime friends is the author of this book. Read it, process it, and get moving for the end-time harvest!

Larry Stockstill

CHAPTER ONE

God's Callings And Commission

"For ye see your calling, brethren, how that not many wise men after the flesh, not many mighty, not many noble, are called: But God hath chosen the foolish things of the world to confound the wise; and God hath chosen the weak things of the world to confound the things which are mighty; And base things of the world, and things which are despised, hath God chosen, yea, and things which are not, to bring to nought things that are: That no flesh should glory in his presence." I Corinthians 1:26-29.

I rejoice that God has called and chosen the foolish things of the world to confound the wise. God calls out the nobodies to make them a somebody in His Kingdom. In the spring of 1968, God called me out of the world and translated me into the kingdom of His dear Son. He called me out of despair and darkness and into His marvelous light and life. I am still rejoicing over His goodness and His great deliverance.

In the spring of 1968, I was a production supervisor at Air Products in east New Orleans. At the young age of twenty-eight I had been successful in my vocation and was up for a promotion as an assistant plant manager. However, my spiritual life was null and void but my flesh life was active and sinful. I lived for the night life – parties, lounges, nightclubs, booze and gambling. Any lust of the flesh, you name it, and it was my lifestyle. My carnal saying was, "I live the life I love and I love the life I live."

At the end of one evening shift, I lead several of my men under my supervision to a go-go joint in east New Orleans. We drank and played into the late night and early morning. Before daylight, one of my men drove me home, intoxicated and dead in my sins. That afternoon, Mary my wife left home with our first two children vowing not to return. She was frustrated and exhausted from living with a drunken husband and a delinquent father. At four that afternoon I was bathing and recovering from the effects of alcohol. In the bathtub, the Holy Spirit visited me with a conviction of sin. Under His conviction, I uttered a short sinner's prayer, "Lord, help me!" As I did, the Holy Spirit revealed three areas of repentance: the nightclubs had to go; the drinking had to stop, and I had to forsake the lust of gambling. For just a moment, I hesitated; these were three habitual pleasures of my carnal life. However, I considered the wages of these sins: a broken down physical body, financial lack and debt, and a divided home with a broken hearted wife. I made a decision. I said to myself, "It's not worth it." I repented and surrendered to the lordship of Christ Jesus and in that very moment I was born-again, regenerated. I went from darkness to light, from selfishness to unselfishness. The cursing stopped; the desire for the party life and alcohol left and the gambling lust took wings. On that April afternoon on 1968, Rod Aguillard became a free man, a godly husband and father, and a believer committed to a local church.

During my first year of covenant commitment to Jesus, I devoured the word of God and enjoyed the fellowship and outreach of my local church body. I became training union director, part-time youth pastor, part of the weekly visitation team, and was overseeing maintenance of the church grounds at no monetary expense to the pastor.

Toward the end of my first year, the Holy Spirit visited me with a calling. In a vision of the night, I saw that I was lying on my face by a river, trembling as I saw the form of God in the firmament. Out of this visitation God ordained me into the ministry as Reverend Rod Aguillard. In the vision, He showed me church buildings, representing the local church assembly. Then I saw myself loving a group of people, going to each one greeting and shaking hands. I knew this was a pastoral call. Later, I discerned that there was more to the vision than a pastoral mandate.

I was reading through the bible when as I came to Ezekiel 1:1 *"Now it came to pass in the thirtieth year, in the fourth month, in the fifth day of the month, as I was among the captives by the river of Chebar, that the heavens were opened, and I saw visions of God."* In the vision of my calling I was by a river and I saw a vision of God.

And then, Ezekiel 1:26-28 *"And above the firmament that was over their heads was the likeness of a throne, as the appearance of a sapphire stone: and upon the likeness of the throne was the likeness as the appearance of a man above upon it. And I saw as the colour of amber, as the appearance of fire round about within it, from the appearance of his loins even upward, and from the appearance of his loins even downward, I saw as it were the appearance of fire, and it had brightness round about. As the appearance of the bow that is in the cloud in the day of rain, so was the appearance of the brightness round about. This was the appearance of the likeness of the glory of the LORD. And when I saw it, I fell upon my face, and I heard a voice of one that spake"* In the vision of my calling, I saw God on a throne and I fell on my face trembling and the voice of God spoke to me ordaining me into the ministry. In other words, at my calling, I received an Ezekiel mantle to be a prophet to the nation and a prophet to the body. A prophetic mantle was released to me at my calling; I did not ask for it, it was the Father's choice and His good will.

As a Baptist believer I was not taught that there was the office of a prophet. In 1970, I obeyed my call to the ministry and went to the New Orleans Baptist Seminary for training. Also, in my seminary training, I was not taught that there was an office of a prophet or an apostle. In that same year, I became the senior pastor of a mission's church in the small community of Reserve, Louisiana, twenty-five miles west of New Orleans. In 1974, we had a visitation of the Holy Spirit on our Baptist church body. Four years of hard work the congregation had grown from thirty to one hundred and thirty. When the baptism of the Holy Spirit fell, we went from one hundred and thirty to thirty, reverse growth or better said, reverse lost.

Out of the rubble, the Holy Spirit began to build a great work or church for His Kingdom. By 1976, we had gained back more than we lost and the move of God was on. Through small groups and prophetic preaching, we exploded in a congregation of three hundred plus. In 1982, we built a debt free sanctuary seating seven hundred forty three, and the Holy Spirit filled it.

It was in 1984 or 1985, that God sent the prophets to my ministry. Under their leadership, my prophetic mantle began to develop. By 1986, I was experiencing the office of the seer. *"I will stand upon my watch, and set me upon the tower, and will watch to see what he will say unto me, and what I shall answer when I am reproved. And the LORD answered me, and said, write the vision, and make it plain upon tables, that he may run that readeth it. For the vision is yet for an appointed time, but at the end it shall speak, and not lie: though it tarry, wait for it; because it will surely come, it will not tarry."* Habakkuk 2:1-2.

As a seer, I began to see the judgments of God upon

our nation due to immorality and the murder of the unborn children or the shedding of innocent blood. During a time of united prayer and fasting for the life of the unborn, the Holy Spirit spoke: "God's bow was bent and His arrow of judgment was pointed toward our nation because of the shedding of innocent blood." He said, "Abortion must stop and you must stop it." Not long after this prophetic word, our local church went to the streets to walk and pray before the abortion mills.

In 1988, we joined the Rescue movement lead by Randall Terry to take a united national stand against the abortion holocaust. Through our efforts, hundreds of abortion mills have closed and tens of thousands of unborn babies have been rescued from the knife of the abortionist. For this accomplishment, we give glory to God!

As a prophetic trumpet alerting the Body to the murder of the unborn, I began to see judgments against our nation. Jeremiah the prophet was asked the question: *"What seest thou?"* Jeremiah 1:11. Of course, Jeremiah began to see the judgments of God against the wickedness of His people who had forsaken Him and burned incense to other gods and worshipped the works of their own hands. *"And I will utter my judgments against them touching all their wickedness, who have forsaken me, and have burned incense unto other gods, and worshipped the works of their own hands."* Jeremiah 1:16.

In 1985 or 1986, I saw droughts and floods coming on our nation as a judgment of our economy. I saw great fires on the west coast, the Holy Spirit referred to them as firestorms.

A few months later, I read the headlines in our state paper, "Firestorms on the West Coast". Firestorms have cost the west coast probably billions of dollars, another judgment against the economy. I remember the saying of another prophet to the nation, "one day God's judgments will out run our federal money printing presses." In 2011, that prediction was being fulfilled.

In 1988, I had a vision of the hedge of protection being down around our nation. The sins of homosexuality, pornography, drugs and drunkenness, the murder of the unborn had caused God to withdraw His hedge of protection over our great nation. Therefore 9-11 was able to happen. On our soil, we experienced a taste of the great sword judgment when demonized terrorists were able to take down the Twin Towers in New York City and murder over three thousand innocent Americans. The hedge of protection is still down.

Listen to the prophet Ezekiel, *"And I sought for a man among them, that should make up the hedge, and stand in the gap before me for the land, that I should not destroy it, but I found none."* Ezekiel 22:30. The only hope for our nation is a desperate united prayer movement that would repent, push back the darkness and open the heavens of revival and moral reformation. I am in over twenty states preaching the gospel to about thirty-five churches. At present, there does not seem to be any desperate prayer movement to stay God's judgment and usher in a move of God that would turn our nation back to righteousness. In the last chapter, I will expound on God's last call for intercessors, a core of God's people that will stand in the gap and raise up the hedge.

As you read, I will discuss in detail the call of the prophet as a trumpet of warning, the stages of God's judgments and our response to the same. *"Shall the trumpet be blown in the city and the people be not afraid? Saying there be evil in the city, and shall not the Lord do something about it."* Amos 3:7. Yes the Lord will and this writing is a warning that His judgments are upon our nation and only the body of Christ can stay it and turn the tables on the principalities and powers.

Chapter Two

The Apostle And The Prophet To The Body

"Now ye are the body of Christ, and members in particular. And God hath set some in the church, first apostles, secondarily prophets, thirdly teachers, after that miracles, then gifts of healings, helps, governments, diversities of tongues." II Corinthians 12:27-28.

"And are built upon the foundation of the apostles and prophets, Jesus Christ himself being the chief corner stone." Ephesians 2:20.

The office of the prophet and the apostle are foundational ministries to the body to bring her into maturity and prepare her for the end of the age. We are moving into the season of final judgments, final revival and the final harvest.

The apostle brings accountability and order to the

body. He imparts vision and structure which results in unity and a wineskin to release the power of God to reach a lost world. *Moving in the Apostolic*, written by John Eckhardt, the author expounds on the importance of the apostle office and his ministry to the local church. Here are several truths he expounds on in his description of the apostle:

1. The Great Commission: *"And Jesus came and spake unto them, saying, All power is given unto me in heaven and in earth. Go ye therefore, and teach all nations, baptizing them in the name of the Father, and of the Son, and of the Holy Ghost: Teaching them to observe all things whatsoever I have commanded you: and, lo, I am with you always, even unto the end of the world. Amen."* Matthew 28:18-20. This is an apostolic commission. In the beginning, it was given to His twelve. Therefore, the Great Commission is an apostolic mandate to bring our Lord's deliverance to all nations. Without apostles, the sent ones, the Great Commission cannot be completed.

2. Commission means to authorize, to appoint, to charge and to empower; it means to entrust with a ministry. The Holy Spirit is the power of the apostles calling and sending. Under this anointing, the apostle has the authority and wisdom to direct evangelism, discipleship, church government, church planting and outreach to the nations of the world.

3. Finally, John Eckhardt pointed out, that the end time commission carries an international anointing to go beyond the communities, cities, and regions of our nation but to

regions beyond…to all people groups throughout the world. The apostles are first in God's order to go to all nations to establish and plant churches. The apostles are first in rank to push back the principalities and powers that have controlled heathen nations for centuries.

Several years ago, Apostle Jim Clark challenged several of us to describe the office of the apostle. I sought the Lord over the challenge and received five streams of the apostolic mantle which are listed as follows:

1. **He is the architect of vision**. Two examples: I have worked closely with Pastor Larry Stockstill from Bethany World Prayer Center. Over a twenty-six year period, Pastor Larry is apostolic as an architect of vision for world missions. In the Global 12 Project now called Surge, he and his team of the International Twelve have planted 10,000 churches in ten years. He is an apostolic visionary with a church planting anointing.

The second example is the Network of Related Pastors (NRP). I am the senior overseer working with ten other apostolic team leaders. We have birthed a vision with several apostolic purposes. We are a fathering-mentoring network; we are raising a prophetic generation of sons and daughters and planting local churches with our sons and daughters. We are being salt, a voice of righteousness into our civil authorities and voice of truth against the murder of the unborn. We are called to fulfill the Great Commission, father missionaries and send sons/daughters to the uttermost parts of the world.

2. **The second stream of the apostolic is training and sending of our sons and daughters to other cities and regions beyond**. For example, NRP is helping to raise up five-fold training centers in the local churches. We have adopted GlobalRoar, a missions training and sending agency in Crown Point, Indiana.

3. **The apostle is anointed to be a father to pastors and actually to all the five-fold ministry and the local body**. I am an apostolic father with a prophetic mantle. The heartbeat of my call is to father-mentor pastors; to affirm them as sons; to be there for them in the storms of life and to help them with order and structure in their local church.

4. **There is a military stream in the apostle's office.** The apostle is the general in the field; the spiritual commander of the church. "Apostolic ministry is a ministry of warfare. It entails commanding, mobilizing, rallying and gathering the army of God to challenge and pull down the strongholds of the enemy. Also, the apostolic anointing releases miracles, healings, signs and wonders that help *destroy strongholds or the mindsets of the lost in regions and nations." Moving in the Apostolic* by John Eckhardt.

5. **The fifth stream of the apostle's office is government.** This apostolic responsibility brings order, structure and accountability to the five-fold ministry and the local church. The power of God came only to those who are in unity under apostolic authority. In Acts 2:1-4, the early church was in one place and in one accord under apostolic

authority and God came by wind and by fire and filled all of the house. And out of that apostolic church, the Lord Himself working through His people turned the world upside down.

Now let us consider the prophet to the body. As scripture teaches, along with the apostle it is a foundational ministry of the local church. Without his office, the purpose and the full anointing and outreach of the local body will not be fulfilled. By the way, the prophet is second in rank to the apostle. He is to flow under the authority of the apostolic father. There are some independent prophets who are really loose cannon balls, not accountable to the apostolic fathers. They have the potential to cause much damage to the church by moving in false prophecy. The prophetic word must be judged by apostolic men and other leaders in the body of Christ. God has an order!

The basic responsibility of the prophet to the body is to give direction and correction. Listed are three truths of understanding the office of the prophet to the body.

1. **He has a builder's permit**. There is a blessing, encouragement, and edification in the prophetic word. *"But he that prophesieth speaketh unto men to edification, and exhortation, and comfort."* I Corinthians 14:3.

The prophet's strategic activity to the body is to build the church by confirming gifts and callings. This is primarily my prophetic flow to the local church, I have a God-given anointing to see gifts and callings on an individual believers life. Recently, I was with Pastor Pacer Hepperly, Church of God, and senior pastor in Maryville, Tennessee. Rio Revolution is in revival and a season of soul winning. In the past four years, they have grown from approximately a hundred people to several hundred. The local body is moving in the "Three E's" of the anointing: Energy, Excitement, and Enthusiasm. Three months ago, January 2011, I did a prophetic summit for his leadership core. The Holy Spirit working through me confirmed the calling and gifting of about fifty key leaders. The prophetic anointing released them into a new level of excitement and harvest. People were being saved during the worship; seventy were saved in one month following the prophetic summit. Recently, the pastor called me to give reports of fresh oil and explosive growth. They are getting ready to build a new facility for the harvest. Last week, April of 2011, a visitor gave a $46,000 check for the new building, sounds like revival has come to Rio Revolution. The Bible described the building and confirming activity of the prophets office: *"Now there were in the church that was at Antioch certain prophets and teachers; as Barnabas, and Simeon that was called Niger, and Lucius of Cyrene, and Manaen, which had been brought up with Herod the tetrarch, and Saul. As they ministered to the Lord, and fasted, the Holy Ghost said, Separate me Barnabas and Saul for the work whereunto I have called them. And when they had fasted and prayed, and laid their hands on them, they sent them away."* Acts 13:1-3.

2. **Secondly, the prophet's word to the body or to the individual is strategic and long term versus a short**

term emotional surge. For example, I received a word over my life and ministry by Prophet Clem Ferris, June 17, 2008. Apparently, most of that word is strategic and long term:

- God said that there is yet another strategic, divine partnership for the kingdom that is going to astound me. It will release young men and funding. This has not happened but will.

- God said that the bane of my ministry is there has never been enough. God said, that is just about to change, plentiful resources are coming. Also, I will help pastors to see God as their abundant provider. This has not happened but will.

- God said that I am an apostle with prophetic stuff all over me. God has given me a releasing mechanism to impart and impact young men and women. This is happening, glory to God! There were at least two other prophetic words that is still strategic and long term and it will happen in God's time. The scripture teaches that the prophet's word has a long term strategy.

> *"Neglect not the gift that is in thee, which was given thee by prophecy, with the laying on of the hands of the presbytery. Meditate upon these things; give thyself wholly to them; that thy profiting may appear to all."* I Timothy 4:14-15.

> *"This charge I commit unto thee, son Timothy, according to the prophecies which went before*

on thee, that thou by them mightest war a good warfare." I Timothy 1:18.

3. Finally, the prophet's word is conditional based on two responses.

First, you must go on to know the Lord. *"Then shall we know, if we go on to know the Lord: His going forth is as certain as the dawn: and He shall water you even as the latter and former rains water the earth."* Hosea 6:3. I have a file filled with the prophet's word over people I pastored during a thirty seven year tenure. So many, too many of those prophetic words will never be fulfilled because they are no longer serving God or flowing with a local church body. Their potential for the kingdom will be buried in their graves: unfulfilled dreams, songs, gifting, and ministry…all because they have fallen out of the kingdom, over an offense or the love of the world.

Secondly, as a disciple you must stay accountable to your senior pastor and the local leadership team. Hebrews 13:7 is still for the church of today: *"obey them that have the rule over you and submit yourself for they watch for your souls."* When I do a prophetic summit for a local church I make it clear to those I am working over, "you must be a man or woman under authority. You are not called to be a mere church member but a disciple or a son or daughter committed to the pastor's heart and the vision of the house." Individuals that are not in this flow will not receive much under the prophet's word. In other words, I will not have much to say unless they are under authority and ready to function in their place of gifts and callings. Then in the last part of Hebrews 13:7 *"...the Holy Spirit exhorts the believer to be under spiritual authority because they must give an account for your soul before the father that they may do it with joy and no with grief, for that is unprofitable for you if you bring grief."*

What a responsibility for the local senior pastor to watch over, feed and lead believers and then give an eternal account for believers who are under their ministry. What an awesome responsibility of the individual believer to come under and submit to their assigned spiritual authority as unto the Lord. God help both of us!

Chapter Three

The Prophet: The Seer To The Nation

"I will stand upon my watch, and set me upon the tower, and will watch to see what he will say unto me, and what I shall answer when I am reproved. And the LORD answered me, and said, Write the vision, and make it plain upon tables, that he may run that readeth it. For the vision is yet for an appointed time, but at the end it shall speak, and not lie: though it tarry, wait for it; because it will surely come, it will not tarry." Habakkuk 2:1-3.

In the prophet's mantle there is a divine ability to hear and see what God is saying and the unction to declare it or write the vision on a tablet. The prophet Habakkuk described his anointing to see what God is saying: *"I will stand upon my watch to see what He will say unto me..."* Habakkuk 2:1.

As I shared earlier, in 1988 I saw a vision of the map of

the United States with the hedge of protection that surrounded us was down. The rebellion in our land, adultery and divorce, gross sexual immorality, and the murder of unborn children were major sins that withdrew God's hand of protection over our nation. God has a lawsuit against our nation. Listen to the words of Hosea the prophet: *"Hear the word of the LORD, ye children of Israel: for the LORD hath a controversy with the inhabitants of the land, because there is no truth, nor mercy, nor knowledge of God in the land."* Hosea 4:1. Because there is a lack of truth and the move of God in our land, there is a spirit of lawlessness. *"By swearing, and lying, and killing, and stealing, and committing adultery, they break out, and blood toucheth blood."* Hosea 4:2. The following list of Hosea 4:2 describes the lawlessness in America:

1. **Swearing** is the violation of the fourth commandment, no respect for the name of the Lord. The GD's of Hollywood are now part of our culture.

2. **Lying** is the violation of the ninth commandment, no respect for integrity. The government leaders of our nation have been caught in one lie after another.

3. **Killing** is the violation of the eighth commandment, no respect for human life. There is murder in the abortion mills, murder in the streets and murder in our schools.

4. **Stealing** is the violation of the eighth commandment, no respect for personal property. There is an epidemic of stealing in our cities and even in our small communities.

5. **Adultery** is the violation of the seventh commandment, no respect for the marriage bed. Adultery and divorce are more the rule for marriages, other than the exception.

6. **One murder follows another murder**: Over 55,000,000 unborn babies have been murdered since the infamous 1973 Roe V. Wade Supreme Court decision. Now, a spirit of murder has been released in our land. Our cities have become war zones where murder in the streets is a common happening. The prophet blows the trumpet against the spirit of lawlessness and calls out to the church to repent and be the salt of the earth. If the church fails to respond in united prayer and a voice of righteousness, then God's judgments begin to be released, *"Therefore shall the land mourn, and every one that dwelleth therein shall languish, with the beasts of the field, and with the fowls of heaven; yea, the fishes of the sea also shall be taken away."* Hosea 4:3.

The prophet to the nation is a predictor; he sees things to come. In the late winter of 1993, I saw a great flood coming to our nation. I declared the vision to the church body that I was pastoring in Reserve, Louisiana. This seeing came to pass from April to October of 1993. It is referred to as the Great Flood of 1993. Quoted from Wikipedia, the free encyclopedia, "The Great Flood of 1993 occurred in the American Midwest, along the Mississippi and Missouri rivers and their tributaries, from April to October 1993. The flood was among the most costly and devastating to ever occur in the United States, with

$15 billion in damages. The hydrographic basin affected cover around 745 miles in length and 435 mile in width, totaling about 320,000 square miles. Within this zone, the flooded area totaled around 30,000 square miles and was the worst such United States disaster since the Great Mississippi flood of 1927, as measured by duration, square miles inundated, persons, displaced, crop and property damage, and number of record river levels. In some categories, the 1993 flood even surpassed the 1927 flood, at the time of the largest flood ever recorded on the Mississippi."

Even as I write, May 15, 2011, five southern states including Louisiana are facing destructive floods from a rising river. Again, it is at a greater flood stage than the Great Flood of 1927. Another national disaster that will cost billions of dollars in lost crops and properties. I am convinced that is part of the judgment called "The breaking of the staff of bread." We are in a slow death of our economy. The printing presses of our federal government cannot keep up with the natural disasters. We are running out of money, our economy is falling and failing.

But God. Listen to the God of hope: *"If I shut up heaven that there be no rain, or if I command the locusts to devour the land, or if I send pestilence among my people; If my people, which are called by my name, shall humble themselves, and pray, and seek my face, and turn from their wicked ways; then will I hear from heaven, and will forgive their sin, and will heal their land."* II Chronicles 7:13-14.

To see the heart of the prophet, you must first

understand of the nature of God's judgments. First of all, God's judgments are unsearchable. *"O the depth of the riches both of the wisdom and knowledge of God! how unsearchable are his judgments, and his ways past finding out!"* Romans 11:33. This comes in the context of Israel being drawn back to God after two thousand plus years, and judgment is a part of God's plan to bring her back. (Read Zechariah chapter 12-14, to see God's dealings with His ancient people.)

We cannot understand all the judgments of God but I will set down several truths that will help you know what He is doing in the judgments of nations as we move into the end of the age. Also, it will help you to see the prophet's heart-felt burden.

1. First, truth in understanding the nature of His judgments: **God's throne is established in righteousness and justice.**

"Say among the heathen that the LORD reigneth: the world also shall be established that it shall not be moved: he shall judge the people righteously." Psalms 96:10

"Clouds and darkness are round about him: righteousness and judgment are the habitation of his throne." Psalms 97:2

God is justice! He will visit the sins of a nation. *"Thus saith the LORD unto this people, Thus have they loved to wander, they have not refrained their feet, therefore the LORD doth not accept them; he will now remember their iniquity, and visit their sins."* Jeremiah 14:10. Humans are eternal; they will face their sins in eternity. The lost will face Him at the Great White Throne judgment. As believers, we will face Him at the judgment seat of Christ giving an account for how we served Him: some for rewards, and for others, their self-centered life will be burned away – still saved, but no rewards. However, nations are temporal and the sin of a nation is dealt within the nasty now: the fall of the Roman Empire, the judgment of Nazi Germany, and Imperial Japan are examples of God judging the sins of a nation.

There are specific sins that will invoke God's judgment on a nation. Listed are three specific sins:

- **The shedding of innocent blood and idolatry.** *"Moreover the word of the LORD came unto me, saying, Son of man, when the house of Israel dwelt in their own land, they defiled it by their own way and by their doings: their way was before me as the uncleanness of a removed woman. Wherefore I poured my fury upon them for the blood that they had shed upon the land, and for their idols wherewith they had polluted it: And I scattered them among the heathen, and they were dispersed through the countries: according to their way and according to their doings I judged them."* Ezekiel 36:16-19. The United States has shed the innocent blood of 55,000,000 unborn babies. This national sin makes us ripe for judgment to satisfy the justice of God. Also, as a nation, we have idols in our heart: sex addictions, sports focus, drinks, drugs, and others like these.

- **The fullness of pride.** *"Behold, this was the iniquity of thy sister Sodom, pride, fullness of bread, and abundance of idleness was in her and in her daughters, neither did she strengthen the hand of the poor and needy. And they were haughty, and committed abomination before me: therefore I took them away as I saw good."* Ezekiel 16:49-50. Pride is the sin of not depending or honoring the lordship of Jesus. It is self-sufficiency, self-indulgence, and living as though God doesn't exist. The Ten Commandments have been made illegal in our government and schools; public prayer in Jesus' name is forbidden. There is an ongoing move to take "In God We Trust" off our money. God is visiting the sin of our pride: *"And the pride of Israel doth testify to his face: therefore shall Israel and Ephraim fall in their iniquity: Judah also shall fall with them. They shall go with their flocks and with their herds to seek the LORD; but they shall not find him; he hath withdrawn himself from them."* Hosea 5:5-6.

- **The sin of forsaking the living God and hewing out cisterns that can hold no water.** *"For my people have committed two evils; they have forsaken me the fountain of living waters, and hewed them out* *cisterns, broken cisterns, that can hold no water."* Jeremiah 2:13. As a whole, our nation has forsaken the living God and our righteous foundation that made us a great nation. We have hewed out cisterns that can hold no water – the broken cisterns of humanism, materialism, and socialism. God help us to return to our roots or suffer the consequences and become a third-world nation.

2. Second truth in understanding God's judgment: **He is Holy.** *The Lord GOD hath sworn by his holiness, that, lo, the days shall come upon you, that he will take you away with hooks, and your posterity with fishhooks."* Amos 4:12. This speaks of judgment being pronounced against Judah *"... He has sworn by His holiness."* Holiness is heavy; it means separation and purity. God is holy: there is no selfishness in God, there is no pride or lust in God. He is untainted by sin. God is the Father of Lights; there is no shadow in God. There is no darkness in God; no, not any at all. Every good and perfect gift comes from above; He is holy. (Paraphrased from James 1:17) *"Speak unto all the congregation of the children of Israel, and say unto them, Ye shall be holy: for I the LORD your God am holy."* Leviticus 19:2. The Hebrew meaning in this context means sacred. God is saying, "I am sacred; I am set apart; I am hallowed; I am the honored one."

In other places in the Old Testament, He is referred to as "the Holy One!" This means, He is the one who cannot tolerate a continual state of unrighteousness (as in the United

States of America). So in understanding His judgments, you must understand His nature; He is holy and He cannot tolerate a spirit of lawlessness in our land. He must eventually balance the scales. His great name in our nation will be sanctified. This is why God is shaking our nation and the nations of the world in this present hour.

3. The third principle in understanding our Father's judgments: **In every nation, God will eventually exonerate His great name**. Yes Father, in Jesus name, do it!

"I will show the holiness of my great name, which has been profaned among the nations, the name you have profaned among them. Then the nations will know that I am the LORD, declares the Sovereign LORD, when I am proved holy through you before their eyes." Ezekiel 36:23.

Since the birth of the United States, we have been that city set on a hill. We have been a Christian nation that lifted up the name of Jesus. We have been a beacon of light and freedom for all nations. This nation has been known as a Christian nation throughout the world. However, in the last five decades, we have profaned and rejected the name of Jesus. But God will have the last word. He will sanctify His great name.

We now see that judgment is the expression of God's justice. It vindicates His character before all the world that He is a holy God and that He does not tolerate the pollution of wickedness and sin in a nation, especially one that has been called by His name. In God's judgment, He will always balance the scales. The psalmist says, *"Commit thy way unto the Lord, trust in Him, and He will bring forth thy righteousness as the light and thy justice as the noonday."* Psalms 96:2. That is the nature of God. He will see that justice is done, whether on my behalf, your behalf, or on the behalf of His great name. From this we see that holiness demands justice. God must establish justice in His dealings with man because the foundation of His throne is righteousness and judgment. The most perfect illustration of this is in the cross of Christ. The heart of the cross is that it is a place of justice, God's great judgment for everyone in the earth to see.

"Therefore by the deeds of the law there shall no flesh be justified in His sight: for by the law is the knowledge of sin. But now the righteousness of God without the law is manifested, being witnessed by the law and the prophets. Whom God hath set forth to be a propitiation through faith in His blood, to declare his righteousness for the remission of sins that are past, through the forebearance of God; To declare, I say at this time His righteousness: that He might be just and the justifier of him which believeth in Jesus." Romans 3:20, 21, 25-26.

We must have a clear understanding of the terms "propitiation" and the "wrath of God." Propitiation means to pacify or appease the wrath of God. It means to satisfy the justice of God. When the wrath of God is appeased, the scales are balanced. In the blood sacrifice of Jesus, sinful man can now come to God and be reconciled. God does not violate His purity, His holiness, or His justice. You must understand the wrath of God. It means this: God is angry at sin; God hates sin. Why? Because He is the Holy One, the One who cannot tolerate a state of unrighteousness. He hates sin because His nature is holiness. *"God is light… in Him there is no darkness, no not none at all…"* I John 1:5. It is a double negative in the Greek. There is only purity and light in God. He hates sin because it gives the devil the legal right to steal, to kill and to destroy humans made in God's image.

Therefore, He cannot tolerate man in his rebellious sin. With this understanding, verse 25 of Romans 3 says that God provided a way to judge man and satisfy justice. How did He satisfy justice? How did He judge man's sin? *"He was wounded for our transgressions, He was bruised for our iniquities; the judgment of our peace was upon Him."* Isaiah 53:4**.** Great plan! No human mind could think of a plan like this. This is the unsearchable judgments of God. Isaiah 53:10 said that it pleased the Lord to bruise Him. Why? To make His soul an offering for sin. In other words, Jesus took the wrath of God; He took God's judgment for our sin once and forever. If you want to see God's justice and righteousness, look at the cross.

At the cross, God is saying I love you and I forgive you even more; God is saying I pardon you and I justify you through the justice satisfied by My Son. The cross is a place of justice; God punished the sins of ungodly sinners in His own Son. Jesus died not for His sins but for our sins. Daniel, the prophet, said that after threescore and two weeks shall Messiah be cut off, but not for Himself. At the cross, the scales of God were balanced for all of mankind, *"that whosoever believeth on Him shall not perish but have everlasting life."* John 3:16.

4. A fourth truth in understanding the nature of His judgments: **God's judgments are stored up for a time and a season.** He does not forget to deal with a nation's sin: immorality, murder, violence and other expressions of lawlessness. Eventually, He will visit the sins of a nation. God is long-suffering; the wheels of His judgments move slowly and only happen after the prophets have warned us over and over. A good example is found in II Samuel 21:1-9. There was a famine during David's reign that lasted three years. David asked the Lord why? The Lord said, *"Then there was a famine in the days of David three years, year after year; and David enquired of the LORD. And the LORD answered, It is for Saul, and for his bloody house, because he slew the Gibeonites"* II Samuel 21:1.

"And the king called the Gibeonites, and said unto them; (now the Gibeonites were not of the children of Israel, but of the remnant of the Amorites; and the children of Israel had sworn unto them: and Saul sought to slay them in his zeal to the children of Israel and Judah.) Wherefore David said unto the Gibeonites, What shall I do for you? and wherewith shall I make the atonement, that ye may bless the inheritance of the LORD?" II Samuel 21:2-3.

The Gibeonites responded to King David's request, *"And they answered the king, The man that consumed us, and that devised against us that we should be destroyed from remaining in any of the coasts of Israel, Let seven men of his sons be delivered unto us, and we will hang them up unto the LORD in Gibeah of Saul, whom the LORD did choose. And the king said, I will give them."* II Samuel 21:5-6. David gave the Gibeonites seven sons of Saul and they were killed on a hill before the Lord. II Samuel 21:9. Once the bodies of the seven sons and the bones of Saul and Jonathan were buried in the tomb of Kish *"and after that, God ended the famine in the land."* II Samuel 21:14.

Think about it, as a nation, we have murdered 55,000,000 unborn babies. Their innocent blood is crying out for justice. The wheels of God's judgment against this rebellious and murderous holocaust have moved slowly. However, we are in the midst of the breaking of the staff of bread and the great sword judgment. I believe that the United States entered into the day of reckoning and accountability, as it was in King David's nation.

5. The fifth truth in understanding God's judgment and seeing the prophet's heart: **God's judgments are redemptive.** The Father's heart is to redeem and to reconcile all men.

"With my soul have I desired thee in the night; yea, with my spirit within me will I seek thee early: for when thy judgments are in the earth, the inhabitants of the world will learn righteousness." Isaiah 26:9.

The innocent blood of the unborn babies cries out for judgment; the blood of Jesus cries out for mercy. The word is clear – God rejoices over mercy more than judgment. His judgments on our nation are a call to the body of Christ to stand in the gap with repentance and cry out for mercy to bring our nation back to God.

CHAPTER FOUR

The Redemptive Nature Of God's Judgment

"With my soul have I desired thee in the night; yea, with my spirit within me will I seek thee early: for when thy judgments are in the earth, the inhabitants of the world will learn righteousness."
Isaiah 26:9.

In the early 1990's, I had a vision of New Orleans being ten to fifteen feet under water. I announced it to my local church, and since we were only about eighteen miles west of New Orleans, most of us bought flood insurance. In the vision, I knew this was a judgment of God to bring the most wicked city in our nation to repentance. In 2005, this judgment came to pass as Hurricane Katrina flooded most of New Orleans with ten to fifteen feet of water. I am only aware of one major church leader in the affected area that preached a message of repentance to turn to God for forgiveness and a revival of righteousness. Pastor Mike Millé of White Dove Fellowship, dressed in a sack cloth, thundered the word of the Lord that God was calling the church to repentance to bring in the power of God for recovery and restoration. No one heeded the word of judgment, repentance and righteousness; rather, the word received was that God is love and had nothing to do with the flooding and the tragic loss of home, property and life. Again, most of the church world fails to see the redemptive nature of God's judgment. As a prophetic voice, I will devote some scriptural understanding to this truth seen throughout world history until the end of the age.

In God's judgments, it is His will that no man should perish. He is long-suffering. Joel, said *"Rend your heart and not your garments and turn to the Lord, for He is gracious, merciful, and slow to anger, and of great kindness."* Joel 2:13. That describes God's nature, that even His judgments are redemptive. *"The Lord is not slack concerning his promise, as some men count slackness; but is longsuffering to us-ward, not willing that any should perish, but that all should come to repentance"* II Peter 3:9. It is God's heart and will that no man should perish. He is patient with fallen man. He is gracious and merciful, slow to anger and of great kindness. If that were not so, we would all be without hope. How many times have you pouted, fumed and complained, yet through it all, realized and received God's forgiveness?

Jesus came to save, not to destroy. When He was not received in Samaria, James and John saw it and said, "Lord, wilt Thou have us to command the fire to come down from heaven and consume them as Elias did?" He rebuked them and said, *"You know not what manner of spirit you are, for the Son of man is not come to destroy lives, but to save them."* Luke 9:55-56. It is never God's will to destroy nations. It only happens when a people refuse Him and reject His forgiveness and warnings of desolating judgment.

As the Second Coming approaches, we must understand the redemptive nature of His judgment. For example, the words recorded in James 5:7 *"Be patient therefore, brethren, unto the coming of the Lord. Behold the husbandman waiteth for the precious fruit of the earth, and hath long patience for it, until he receive the early and latter rain"* We know through prophecy that the early rain was the Pentecostal rain in Acts 2, when God first poured out His Holy Spirit. The latter rain began sometime at the turn of this century, when God began to pour out His Spirit to make ready the final harvest.

He is coming again as the Judge. However, even in the great judgments of tribulation, God desires men to repent. The Revelator describes the trumpet judgments, at mid-tribulation when the great judgments are about to begin, and the seventh seal has been broken – *"and the rest of the men which were not killed by these plagues yet repented not of the works of their hands, that they should not worship devils, and idols of gold, and silver, and brass, and stone, and of wood: which neither can see, nor hear, nor walk: Neither repented they of their murders, nor of their sorceries, nor of their fornication, nor of their thefts."* Revelation 9:20-21. They still had the opportunity to repent. Man is in the height of rebellion. The judgments are fierce and destructive, yet the majority is still resisting Jesus as Lord.

There are three redemptive principles of God's judgment:

The first was stated earlier: All of God's judgments are to bring men to repentance and righteousness. *"With my soul have I desired Thee in the night: yea, with my spirit within me will I seek Thee early: for when Thy judgments are in the earth, the inhabitants of the world will learn righteousness."* Isaiah 26:9. You can see from this scripture that God had redemption in His judgments. The judgments of God will strip man of his self-sufficiency and his prosperity, and will cause him to turn to God. They tell me that in World War II, churches in America were filled. God said that He has chosen the poor to be rich in faith. The poor man is the humble man. The poor man realizes that without God he can do nothing, and often judgments must come to produce that in a man's heart.

The second principle of redemption in God's judgment is that God raises and destroys nations based on their commitment and goodness. *"O house of Israel, cannot I do with you as this potter? Saith the Lord. Behold, as the clay is in the potter's hand, so are you in Mine hand, O house of Israel. At what instant I shall speak concerning a nation, and concerning a kingdom, to pluck up , and to pull down, and to destroy it."* Jeremiah 18:6-7. When Jeremiah was called in the first chapter, God commissioned that he would speak, and the word of God spoken through him would actually bring judgment to a nation. *"See, I have this day set thee over the nations and over the kingdoms, to root out, and pull down, and to destroy and to throw down, to build and to plant."* Jeremiah 1:10.

In that commission of Jeremiah, the final part was to build and to plant. By his word, he would actually speak nations into existence and into strength. I am convinced that the Holy Spirit is rejuvenating this same type of ministry in the local church. We will come into that anointing of speaking judgment on nations, and speaking for nations to come forth. That is the authority that we have through His word. Consider this commission of authority given to the body of Christ, *"And I say also unto thee, That thou art Peter, and upon this rock I will build my church; and the gates of hell shall not prevail against it. And I will give unto thee the keys of the kingdom of heaven: and whatsoever thou shalt bind on earth shall be bound in heaven: and whatsoever thou shalt loose on earth shall be loosed in heaven."* Matthew 16:18-19.

Through the Apostle Peter, our Lord Jesus gave Peter the keys of the kingdom of heaven, "keys" representing the authority of God's Kingdom. In the keys, we have the grace to see the will of our Father God and have the authority to release the will of God into planet earth. Therefore, if we would be still and see what the Lord is saying, and seize what He is saying, and then decree what He has said, we would be establishing the will of God into whatever area we are praying for or about. Therefore, with the keys, we actually have the authority to speak Godly men into the high offices of our government. We have the authority to turn the heart of a king or our president. "There is awesome power in prophetic praying that has seen the will and heart of our Father." Mike Bickles, IHOP.

The third principle of God's redemptive judgment is that the fierceness of released judgment continues until righteousness is established. Jeremiah talks about a covenant nation, one that God had ordained for His purposes, but they refused and rebelled.

Also, through the judgment of God, there is a purging and restoration of the church. Judgment must first begin at the house of the Lord. God will use suffering to purge the church. Suffering does not weaken the church; rather, suffering makes her stronger. Suffering is not an enemy of the church, but a friend. Ezekiel talks about the four sore judgments, and a remaining remnant: *"For thus saith the Lord God; How much more when I send My four sore judgments upon Jerusalem, the sword, and the famine, and the noisome beast, and the pestilence, to be cut off from man and beast? Yet behold, therein shall be left a remnant that shall be brought forth, both sons and daughters: behold, they shall come forth unto you, and ye shall see their way and their doings: and ye shall be comforted concerning the evil that I brought upon Jerusalem, even concerning all that I have brought upon it.) And they shall comfort you, when ye see their ways and their doings: and ye shall know that I have not done without cause all that I have done in it, saith the Lord God."* Ezekiel 14:21-22.

When He is finished with these judgments, God says you will see something good happen. You will see why He has done what He has done. It was not mere punishment. It was not meant just to balance the scales. God has something greater than that, He is going to bring forth a righteousness remnant.

When persecution hit the Iron Curtain, Dr. Haralan I. Popov said it was like a purging fire sweeping the church. In that day, the average church under persecution kept about ten percent of the congregation. In other words, when all the pressures did her work, a congregation of five hundred was left with a zealous remnant of fifty. Popov said, "Oh the sweetness of that people. Only the nucleus, the committed few were left who knew Jesus Christ and Him crucified."

The purging of the remnant is described by Isaiah the prophet. *"How is the faithful city become a harlot! It was full of judgment; righteousness lodged in it; but now murderers. Thy silver is become dross, thy wine mixed with water;...And I will restore thy judges as at the first, and thy counselors as at the beginning: afterward thou shalt be called the city of righteousness, the faithful city, Zion shall be redeemed with judgment, and her converts with righteousness."* Isaiah 1:21-27.

Notice how she is going to be redeemed. Again, we see the redemptive nature of God's judgments, restoring a nation back to her original state. I really have hope for this nation that God is going to restore her to a measure of what she once was, at least for a season. I believe it will be a Nineveh-type revival. Nineveh repented and came back to God, and God restored her for a season, but at a later date she was completely betrayed. She went back again into iniquity and was finally brought down by God's judgment. I believe righteousness will be restored at many levels in this nation, but she will defect some place down the line and God will bring her into a terrible judgment and we will lose our place as a world power.

In judgment there is a principle of pressure and discipline in birthing character and revival. The writer of Hebrews pens this in a redemptive sense. The end result of God's pressure and discipline is the peaceable fruit of righteousness. This is God's desire and His will. My children knew me as father and as judge. I judged their wrongdoings. I gave them justice through spankings and recovered them with hugs and kisses. From those spankings, a peaceable fruit of righteousness was born. That is God's principle in dealing with a rebellious nation.

Charles Finney said that revival often comes under three conditions: 1) When the wickedness of the wicked distresses and grieves the Christian church. In this wickedness, God's judgments are in the earth and the church is the first to see it. 2) Seeing this wickedness, and the awesomeness of God's judgments, the church bows in repentance. Judgment comes first to the house of God. 3) Again, seeing the wickedness, the Christian becomes willing to sacrifice his time for prayer, his feelings, and even some of his family time, to help promote revival in the midst of wrath that a nation and generation might be spared.

God will spare His full judgments on a backslidden

nation based on the remnant of consecrated believers. In early redemptive history, God is speaking and Abraham is listening. He has separated himself to God and is walking with God so that he can hear from Him. *"And the Lord said, the cry of Sodom and Gomorrah is great and because their sin is very grievous, I will go down now, and see whether they have done altogether according to the cry of it, which is come unto Me; and if not I will know. And the men turned their faces and thence, and went toward Sodom; but Abraham stood yet before the Lord. And Abraham drew near, and said, Wilt thou also destroy the righteous with the wicked? Peradventure there be fifty righteous within the city: wilt thou also destroy and not spare the place for the fifty righteous that are therein? That be far from thee to do after this manner, to slay the righteous with the wicked: and that the righteous should be as the wicked, that be far from Thee: Shall not the Judge of all the earth do right? And the Lord said, If I find in Sodom fifty righteous within the city, then I will spare all the place for their sakes."* Genesis 18:20-26.

Abraham knew there were not 50 righteous men in Sodom and he brought God down to ten and that is as far as God would go! Theologians believe there were approximately 10,000 people in Sodom. God's bottom line for sparing those 10,000 people was 10 righteous men. That is one man per thousand people who was fervent, salty, really serving God with all his heart. The 2010 USA census was 308,745,538 million people. Based on the ten righteous men ratio, it would take 308,745 consecrated believers to preserve this nation.

The presence of righteous believers is a decisive factor in determining the extent of the judgments of God.

The Lord gave me a vision of God's judgments coming into America. I saw Him judging sections, areas that were void of Christian witness, such as New York City. In this city, one out of every two babies is murdered each day. I saw God desolating certain areas where there is no remnant. A small remnant in Israel spared total desolation as recorded by Isaiah the prophet, *"Except the Lord had left unto us a very small remnant, we should have been as Sodom and we should have been like unto Gomorrah."* Isaiah 1:9. In this hour, the Holy Spirit is working to raise up a small remnant that would partially spare our nation from the judgments recorded in the book of Revelation. Prophets to the nation like Joel are blowing a trumpet of warning calling the body of Christ to repentance and become the salt of the earth to stop the moral decay of our nation.

Chapter Five

The Prophets Warning: God Is At War With Evil

"He that committeth sin is of the devil; for the devil sinneth from the beginning. For this purpose the Son of God was manifested, that he might destroy the works of the devil." I John 3:8.

Three main purposes of our Lord's first coming:

He came to redeem man! *"In whom we have redemption through His blood and the forgiveness of our sins according to the nature of His grace."* Ephesians 1:7. The blood of Jesus Christ redeems the repentive and sets us free over the power of sin, Satan, and selfishness. In Christ Jesus, we are free men – free to love, free to live, free to forgive and free to laugh.

Secondly, He came to reconcile man! *"...To wit, that God was in Christ, reconciling the world unto Himself."* II

Corinthians 5:19. Jesus Christ has reconciled us to the Father; that is, He has brought us back into fellowship and favor with the King of the universe. Out of His favor and fellowship we have dominion over the darkness and have all the blessings and benefits of God's kingdom. The arisen Christ gave the church, the redeemed of the Lord, all authority in heaven and earth. Therefore, we have an anointing to preach the good news, heal the sick, and deliver the captives and disciple nations.

The third purpose of His first coming was to destroy evil. *"for this purpose the son of God was manifest or revealed, that He might destroy the works of the devil."* I John 3:8. He came not only to destroy the power of sin, but to destroy the penalty of sin or the curses of the broken law. The four curses of the broken law are sickness/diseases, mental torment, poverty, and the second death. The first three curses are carried out by demon powers. In the exchange of the cross, Jesus is our healer, our deliverer, and our provider. At the cross He bore our sickness, took on our mental torment and became our poverty, thereby destroying the works of Satan.

Out of our Lord's great victory at Calvary, I have a prophetic word for this generation: God is at war with evil and God has anointed us for war and take over. As I expound on this truth, it is my prayer that it will change and challenge you, and you will see yourself as a warrior confronting evil.

In 2010, the Holy Spirit spoke a prophetic warning to me out of the book of Jeremiah. *"The lion is come up from his thicket, and the destroyer of the Gentiles is on his way; he is gone forth from his place to make my land desolate and thy cities shall be laid in waste, without an inhabitant."* Jeremiah 4:7. The Holy Spirit warned me that certain principalities and powers had entered our nation through open doors of national sin. These particular principalities are now controlling the major gates of influence and are intent on corrupting us from within and destroying us as a civilization. The main goal of darkness is to silence the mouth of the church and destroy her ability to evangelize the world. We are in a war for survival and takeover!

The lion has come out of the thicket: *"the iniquity of the house of Israel and Judah is very great...the land is full of blood."* Ezekiel 9:9. The wickedness of America is very great and our land is full of innocent blood. The infamous Roe v. Wade, 1973, issued this murderous decree: The unborn is not human life and can be terminated by the choice of a would-be mother. In 1973, I was sitting in a Baptist seminary class where the professor asked how many of us agreed with the Supreme Court decision of Roe v. Wade. I sat in utter shock as about eighty percent of the training pastors raised their hands in agreement. Judgment certainly begins at the house of God.

Since the decree of death was legally set in as national law, 55,000,000 unborn children have been murdered in the pregnant womb of would-be mothers. Today, 4,200 will be murdered. In 2011, 1.2 million were violently murdered; their silent screams are heard by our heavenly Father. Their innocent blood is crying out for justice. The bad report is that most of the church world is looking the other way. As the German church responded in the Jewish holocaust, the American church responds in the same manner to the abortion holocaust – yellow silence. Dietrich Bonhoeffer, a German pastor and theologian, was hung by Adolf Hitler for resisting and crying out against the evil of murdering innocent Jews. He made this statement that the leaders of the American church world need to hear, "Not to speak against evil is evil, not to act is to act…" God help the church in America to be the salt of the church and to be at war with evil in every form.

"…The lion has come up from his thicket, and the destroyer of the Gentiles is on His way…" Jeremiah 4:7. God is at war with evil. Socialism is the mindset of a principality. Socialism is evil! Socialism is an Anti-Christ form of government. Nazism got its name from National Socialism. National Socialism is the bed fellow of communism and is all about government take over and is an enemy of freedom. From my readings, "Under Socialism a ruling class of intellectuals, bureaucrats and liberal social planners decide what people want or what they think is good for society. Then out of their pride and deceit, they use the coercive power of the state to regulate (the oil spill moratorium), tax and redistribute the wealth of those who work for a living and to those who won't work (the Democratic Party ever-increasing welfare system)."

Forty-five percent of Americans pay no income tax. Fifty-five percent of Americans work and support forty percent of Americans who are paid *not* to work by the federal government. If we would consider the cost of supporting millions of illegal Mexican immigrants, the percentage of those who pay no taxes would be over fifty percent. President Obama, Harry Reid, Nancy Pelosi and the majority of the Democratic Party are socialist. They are driven by a principality, whose mind set is to destroy America, the land of the free. I cry out to the Lord, "Wake up the church". Let her hear the voice of the prophets to this nation. The lion has come up out of the thicket to destroy our land and silence the church.

Socialism is evil. The majority of Americans and conservative media are baffled why the White House and the current Democratic-ruled Senate are driven toward destructive spending. Government control of healthcare, banking and the car industry, environmental thinking that erodes our economy, ungodly abortion and homosexual rights and many other policies are driving our nation over a cliff into a third world status. It is simple: we are not dealing with personalities; we are a nation being destroyed by principalities. "The lion has come up out of the thicket." A three-headed lion has invaded our nation – Socialism, Islam, and Humanism.

The good news: God is at war with evil! Listen to the prophet Moses, *"Then sang Moses and the children of Israel this song unto the LORD, and spake, saying, I will sing unto the LORD, for he hath triumphed gloriously: the horse and his rider hath he thrown into the sea. The LORD is my strength and song, and he is become my salvation: he is my God, and I will prepare him an habitation; my father's God, and I will exalt him. The LORD is a man of war: the LORD is his name."* Exodus 15:1-3. We serve the Jehovah Nissa, He is the Lord, our man of war! What he was then, He still is now! *"Jesus Christ the same yesterday, and today, and forever."* Hebrews 13:8.

The Holy Ghost is a warrior. Our Lord is not that long-haired, white-face, blue-eyed, sissy-looking Jesus depicted by past and present artist. The Revelator saw Him as a warrior. *"And I saw heaven opened, and behold a white horse; and he that sat upon him was called Faithful and True, and in righteousness he doth judge and make war. His eyes were as a flame of fire, and on his head were many crowns; and he had a name written, that no man knew, but he himself. And he was clothed with a vesture dipped in blood: and his name is called The Word of God. And the armies which were in heaven followed him upon white horses, clothed in fine linen, white and clean. And out of his mouth goeth a sharp sword, that with it he should smite the nations: and he shall rule them with a rod of iron: and he treadeth the winepress of the fierceness and wrath of Almighty God. And he hath on his vesture and on his thigh a name written, KING OF KINGS, AND LORD OF LORDS."* Revelation 19:11-16. Not many pulpits are painting this picture of a Jesus that is at war with evil returning to destroy the Anti-Christ and the nations who follow him. Holy Spirit wake up the pulpits of America: God is at war with evil!

In 1968, I was born from above. I was born into covenant with my Creator, my Redeemer, my King, and my Commander-in-Chief. In Covenant, I am first a son. I have received the spirit of adoption, whereby I cry out to my father in Heaven. Secondly, I am a servant; that is, I live to love and serve God and people. Jesus said that He came not to be served but to serve. I have heard it said, "A leader is better called a servant." I enjoy serving people. I live to love God and to serve people. Join me! Thirdly, in covenant I am anointed to be a warrior. I am anointed to hate evil and to war against evil in every form. I rejoice with the psalmist, *"Blessed be the Lord my strength who teaches my hands to war and my fingers to fight."* Psalms 144:1. Join me; together we are anointed by our man of war to stand against evil and to take over. *"The kingdom of Heaven suffers violence and the violent take it by force...."* Matthew 11:12. "Take it" is an active verb. We must become aggressive and take back what the enemy has stolen from our culture and the church body. All of us are anointed to be bold activist unashamed of Jesus name.

I am going to share five truths that will give you an understanding of evil and see God's call to the body of Christ to confront evil.

First and Foremost Satan is the source of all evil. *"The thief comes only in order to steal and kill and destroy. I came that they may have and enjoy life, and have it in abundance (to the full, till it overflows)"* John 10:10. The amplified version gives the subjunctive tense, it is a potential: the devil may steal, he may kill, he may destroy. The potential depends on our resistance or lack of resistance. Jesus Christ has given us authority over the evil one and he really has no power to hurt us or stop us unless we sin and open doors, or become passive. Again, Satan is the source of all evil. *"Wherein in time past ye walked according to the course of this world, according to the prince of the power of the air, the spirit that now worketh in the children of disobedience."* Ephesians 2:2. I am a use-to-be. I use to walk with hell. Mary, my wife said that in the B.C. days (before Christ) I had four horns and two tails. But God! In 1968, I got born again. Jesus Christ in; the power of darkness out. The two tails are gone; all the horns have been removed. Just one little bump remains on my head as a witness: "look what I was, look at what I am, look what Jesus has done!"

Satan is the source of all evil! In 2010, the Congress of the United States passed a Hate Law Bill; it could be criminal to speak against homosexuals from the pulpit. In the same year, they passed the Department of Defense Bill S3280 which allows open homosexuality in the military and tax paid abortions in all of our military facilities. Our nation has affronted God's righteousness and justice. We are certainly weighed in the balance and found wanting. Recently, I read a reliable news article that Hillary Clinton, along with other U.N. leaders are a part of a U.N. small arms treaty. If ratified by the liberal U.S. Senate; legal action could be taken to confiscate and destroy all unauthorized civilian firearms (by the way, which is contrary to the Bill of Rights, our right to bear arms). Also, it would ban the trade, sale and private ownership of all semi-automatic weapons; again against our constitutional right to bear arms. Finally, it would create an international gun registry, setting the stage for full scale gun confiscation. The unthinkable is happening. The prophetic word is true. *"The lion is come up from his thicket and the destroyer of the Gentiles is on his way…to make the land desolate."* Jeremiah 4:7.

Satan is the source of all evil. National Socialism corrupts our federal government. Our basic freedoms are at risk. The western civilization has forsaken its righteous roots, evil seems to be winning the day. Humanism rules the media and public education. The elitist have taken control of communications. Most of the church world's voice of righteousness and justice has been silenced by our passivity. Jezebel runs Hollywood. The immoral mindset of darkness has overtaken the majority of Americans. And what blinds the lost through immorality, binds much of the church world. Islam threatens war and takeover: the leaders of Islam in our nation are predicting their takeover of America by 2050. It is almost past time for the church to wake up and become salt to our nation. Indeed, the lion has come up out his thicket and is rapidly destroying the foundations that made America great.

The second truth is to understand the problem of evil and to confront evil, God hates evil! *"These six things doth the LORD hate: yea, seven are an abomination unto him: A proud look, a lying tongue, and hands that shed innocent blood, An heart that deviseth wicked imaginations, feet that be swift in running to mischief, A false witness that speaketh lies, and he that soweth discord among brethren."* Proverbs 6:16-19. God hates evil, there is no gray matter in God; He either hates or

He loves. As the writer of Proverbs stated, there are seven things that the Lord hates with a capital H. He hates that proud look, the independent spirit that rejects Christ Jesus as Savior and scorns the church body – the Ted Turners, the Bill Mahers of HBO, the liberal media communicators of CNN, CBS, and ABC. He hates hands that shed innocent blood, the hands of the abortionist, the agenda of Planned Parenthood, the White House and liberal Democrats that support the funding of Planned Parenthood and abortion. God is angry toward this! Are you? God hates those who sow discord among the brethren, who sow discord in the local church and come against the pastoral leadership. As a pastor, I hated the same and confronted the evil-doers that were sowing discord and scattering the young sheep. No one that sows discord in the local church should be allowed to stay unless there is repentance and restoration.

God hates evil! The Apostle John and James declared this truth: *"This then is the message which we have heard of him, and declare unto you, that God is light, and in him is no darkness at all."* I John 1:5. John stated there is no darkness in God, no none at all. There is no evil in God. He is without pride or prejudice. There is no selfishness or lust in God. There is no injustice or unrighteousness in God. James stated, there is no variableness in God. He is constant and does not move from truth. There is no shadow in God; there is no darkness, no shades of truth. There is no deceit in God. He is absolute truth and faithfulness!

Evil is always against the will of the Father. We see

it when the rapist victimizes a woman; it is against the will of the woman and it is against the will of God. It is evil! When the abortionist murders 4,200 unborn children a day, it is against the will of the unborn and against the will of our heavenly Father. Abortion is the product of the devil and a sleeping, silent church. Premature death is evil. It is never the will of our Father. Let's believe His promise, *"The days of our years are threescore years and ten; and if by reason of strength they be fourscore years, yet is their strength labour and sorrow; for it is soon cut off, and we fly away"* Psalms 90:10. On December 11, 2008 my oldest (44 years old) and beautiful daughter took her life coming out of a depressed state. A spirit of depression and suicide took hold of her mind and convinced her that taking her life was the way out. My daughter was not killed by God; she was a casualty of war! The good news, the spirit of suicide said "death" at the moment of her last heart beat, God said, "life". She is in Heaven awaiting her family. Two days after her funeral, the voice of the Holy Spirit spoke *"Do not gloat over me, my enemies! For though I fall, I will rise again. Though I sit in darkness, the* L$_{ORD}$ *will be my light. I will be patient as the* L$_{ORD}$ *punishes me, for I have sinned against him. But after that, he will take up my case and give me justice for all I have suffered from my enemies. The* L$_{ORD}$ *will bring me into the light, and I will see his righteousness."* Micah 7:8-9**.** I have it in my heart; the Lord Himself will give me justice for all that my family and I have suffered at the hand of our enemy. Even now, in my national ministry, there is an increasing release of captives, of deliverance to the mentally oppressed. There is a ministry of comfort to those who are in need of comfort. I am a messenger of hope to the hopeless. Also, my home church is going to build "Lynne's Dream House" to minister to the mentally depressed, 24/7. To God be the glory!

Following is a condensed outline of my basic theology which gives me the foundation on understanding evil and confronting evil. I built this outline of basic warfare theology from a book, "God at War" authored by Gregory A. Boyd.

The Biblical Worldview: Understanding and Confronting Evil:

I. **The Biblical Worldview**

    A. The whole of the cosmos is understood to be caught in a fierce battle between two kingdoms… God's and Satan's.

    B. Therefore, the earth is a fierce war zone between God and evil.

II. **The Religious Worldview** (St. Augustine)

God is controlling evil. All things are coming from the Father's hand…good and evil. God allows evil for a greater good. There is no cosmic war…there are no battles to be fought. We just rest and trust in the providence of God. It is obvious that much of the Protestant church world is influenced by this wrong theology.

III. **Comparing the two views**

   A. **Religious Worldview**: God is controlling evil. (Not true.)

     - **Biblical Worldview**: God is at war with evil.

   B. **Religious Worldview**: God's will is perfectly carried out through evil as well as good. (Not true.)

     - **Biblical Worldview**: The world is a hostage to the evil cosmic source.

   C. **Religious Worldview**: Evil is always and everywhere secretly fulfilling God's sovereign and beneficial purposes. (Not true.)

     - **Biblical Worldview**: Evil is a hostile alien intrusion into God's good and perfect will for mankind.

   D. **Religious Worldview**: We do not resist evil; it is all part of God's providence, and much good and a higher purpose will come out of it… divine fruit and results. Sickness and disease is my cross; death of my son is my cross! (Not true.)

     - **Biblical Worldview**: We are free from trying to explain away evil and tragedy; rather we are empowered to rise up and combat evil on every level. Glory to God; let's do it!

   E. **Religious Worldview**: There are free beings,

humans and angelic, that do such atrocities, but it is carried out under God's divine permission. (Not true; God hates evil.)

- **Biblical Worldview**: Humans are tortured and killed; women are raped and murdered because free beings, human and angelic, can and will do such atrocities.

F. **Religious Worldview**: The sovereign God has willed the evil because through it, He is working out a higher purpose or reason. (Not true. Again, God hates evil.)

- **Biblical Worldview**: While the sovereign God can work some good out of horrifying demonic events, the evil itself can only exist because free beings who are against God have willed it and carried it out. (The terrorists and Twin Towers are examples.)

G. **Biblical Worldview** is more responsible than religious because it opens our eyes to the reality of war with evil and our responsibility to know our weapons of warfare and to fight or resist or push back the darkness. And at the same time, it offers hope. We can cast out devils; we can heal the sick. We can deliver the mentally tormented; we can set captives free and open the blind eyes of the lost. We can take cities and take regions…and regions beyond. Let's do it!

IV. **In the Biblical Worldview**, the cross and resurrection, first and foremost, was a defeat in principle of Satan's evil kingdom. As the Body, we live in warfare terms because the fatally wounded kingdom of darkness still does evil in the earth.

Therefore, we must enforce the victory of the cross and resurrection within our personal family life and church Body life. Then we must enforce it to rescue the perishing …(binding and loosing…the keys of the kingdom).

The third truth in understanding the problem of evil: When Jesus came, He confronted evil throughout His ministry. Read His commission and His anointing. *"The Spirit of the Lord is upon me, because he hath anointed me to preach the gospel to the poor; he hath sent me to heal the brokenhearted, to preach deliverance to the captives, and recovering of sight to the blind, to set at liberty them that are bruised, To preach the acceptable year of the Lord."* Luke 4:18-19.

Most of the good news of His earthly ministry had to do with confronting evil. He healed the broken-hearted; He delivered the captive of demons; He brought sight to the blind and the healing of every sickness and disease; He set at liberty those that were crushed and bruised by the powers of darkness. By the anointing, Jesus Christ delivered people from the curses of the broken law – sickness and disease, poverty, mental oppression or mental illness. These curses were and are inflicted by demon powers. Therefore, where Jesus came, He first and foremost confronted and broke the power of evil. Someone said, "that everywhere Jesus went, hell broke beneath His feet." *"How God anointed Jesus of Nazareth with the Holy Ghost and with power: who went about doing good, and healing all that were oppressed of the devil; for God was with him."* Acts 10:38.

Again, the good news of our Lord's first coming to earth, He went about tearing down the evil tyranny of victimized human beings. As the head was and the head is, so should be His body. You have, we have, the same commission and the same anointing to go about healing and delivering the captives. To this end, we most consecrate ourselves and separate from a world system that is carnal, secular and sensual. Let's do it!

The fourth truth in understanding and confronting evil: God enjoins us to hate evil with Him. *"You who love the Lord, hate evil!"* Psalms 97:10. The fear of the Lord is to hold God in awe, that is, the Almighty, the Creator of heaven and earth, our Redeemer, and the Holy and Eternal One. *"The fear of the Lord is to love God with all thy heart, with all thy soul and with all thy mind."* Matthew 22:37. *"The fear of the Lord is to hate evil and to love righteousness."* Proverbs 8:13. The fear of the Lord is to hate what breaks our heavenly Father's heart. The fear of the Lord is to hate hands that shed innocent blood or to hate abortion enough to stand against it as a voice of righteousness, to go to the halls of Congress in protest or go to the streets in front of the abortion mills with intercession and a release of God's judgment against the same. By the way, it breaks the Father's heart to see Jezebel and those under its influence sow discord to divide His body and scatter His sheep. The list of evil that God hates is almost endless – drug trafficking, prostitution of young girls, molestation, pornography, idolatry, and gambling to name a few. Whatever destroys human life, His creation, God hates. My main prophetic calling in confronting evil is to be a voice of righteousness against the murder of the unborn children.

To hate evil is to confront evil. In 1986, the Holy Spirit laid it on my heart to take street action against the shedding of innocent blood. I, along with my leadership team, began to watch the civil rights movement led by Martin Luther King. I was deeply impressed with his courage and his conviction, and his non-violent resistance to free his people from the blight of segregation and the ungodly racist laws of the South. After watching the civil rights series, I began to pray for a Martin Luther King to free the unborn children. In 1988, my prayer was answered, God raised up a New Yorker by the name of Randall Terry who led an anti-abortion, non-violent street movement called "Rescue". For five years, 1988-1992, we were in the streets, having non-violent sit-ins before the abortion mills of America. For the first time in my life, I was arrested and jailed on many occasions, a prisoner for Christ in resisting evil. Because of our efforts in confronting evil, hundreds of abortion mills went out of business; thousands of unborn babies were spared the knife and now live; abortion became a national issue on the political scene and is still the number one social issue in the Federal and State level of government. I am convinced that the seed-bed to overthrow Roe v. Wade was planted by the "rescue" movement.

The fifth truth in confronting evil: you must fight for your heart and connect with warriors who will fight with you on an often basis. In a later part of this book, I will go into detail about keeping your heart and fighting for your heart. For now, here are just a few words concerning the same. If you are born again, the spirit of a champion is in you. You and I have a warriors anointing to stand against evil and to resist personal temptations. By morning, I enforce the victory of Calvary. I take the blood of Jesus for my sin, the cross of Jesus (co-crucifixion) for my selfishness, the scourging of Jesus for my healing and health, and the resurrection of Jesus for my life and anointing. In this, I become a complete person – a witness and a warrior.

In closing, as we confront evil, we must connect with warriors. "Something stronger than fate has chosen you. Evil will hunt you. And so a fellowship must protect you. Honestly, though he is a very brave and true hobbit, Frodo hasn't a chance without Sam, Merry, Pippin, Gandalf, Aragorn, Legolas, and Gimli. He has no real idea what dangers and trials lie ahead. The dark mines of Moria, the Balrog that awaits him there, the evil orcs call the Urak-hai that will hunt him, or the wastes of Emyn Muil. He will need his friends. And you will need yours. You must cling to those you have; you must search wide and far for those you do not yet have. You must not go alone. From the beginning, right there in Eden, the Enemy's strategy has relied upon a simple aim: divide and conquer. Get them isolated, and take them out." (*Waking the Dead* by John Eldredge.)

Chapter Six

Apostolic Fathers: Prophetic Sons And Daughters (The Elisha Generation)

"Behold, I will send you Elijah the prophet before the coming of the great and dreadful day of the LORD: And he shall turn the heart of the fathers to the children, and the heart of the children to their fathers, lest I come and smite the earth with a curse." Malachi 4:5-6.

What time is it? As foretold by the prophets, we are living in the times of refreshing and the restoration of all things. *"Repent ye therefore, and be converted, that your sins may be blotted out, when the times of refreshing shall come from the presence of the Lord."* Acts 3:19. We are living in the times of refreshing. God is coming *to* His church before He comes *for* His church. God is coming to His church as He did on the day of Pentecost. He is coming by wind and by fire.

The Holy Spirit is coming to His church in awesome power and irresistible holiness. We are living in the final fulfillment of Isaiah 60:1-4, *"Arise, shine; for thy light is come, and the glory of the LORD is risen upon thee. For, behold, the darkness shall cover the earth, and gross darkness the people: but the LORD shall arise upon thee, and his glory shall be seen upon thee. And the Gentiles shall come to thy light, and kings to the brightness of thy rising. Lift up thine eyes round about, and see: all they gather themselves together, they come to thee: thy sons shall come from far, and thy daughters shall be nursed at thy side."* We are certainly living in the time of gross darkness or in the final conflict of Hell with Heaven. The beast has come out of the sea and the lion is coming out of the thicket to destroy the land of the brave and the land of the free. The good news: the glory of God is going to fill the local body that is under apostolic authority. And out of our womb, we will birth a manchild, that is our sons and daughters who will push back the powers of darkness and usher in the judgments of God. The prophetic generation of overcomers has been decreed, *"...our sons shall come from far and our daughters shall be nursed at our side."* Isaiah 60:4. This is one of my main purposes as an apostolic father – to raise up a prophetic generation of sons and daughters that will defy the spirit of Anti-Christ.

Secondly, we are living in the time of restoration of all things. The Holy Spirit is working to put the body together in right order. He is restoring us into the original pattern of the New Testament church: apostolic authority, apostolic faith and apostolic power. The Holy Spirit is at work through the body of Christ to climax the end of the age or to usher in the "Day of the Lord."

As we have been taught, we are in the restoration of the entire five-fold ministry: 1970 – the office of the teacher; 1980 – the office of the prophet; 1990 – until present, the office of the apostle. The apostle was the first office to get taken out by the enemy and it is the last office being restored to fully confront our enemy. Just a reminder: the office of the pastor and the evangelist were already functioning offices, even before the turn of this century.

The restoration of the apostolic father is the final key in birthing the all-powerful end-time church that will harvest multitudes and confront the harlot and the beast as revealed in Revelation. In relationship to the apostolic father, the ultimate revelation of the Godhead is the father. *"If you really know me, you will know my Father as well. From now on, you do know him and have seen him."* John 14:7. The Lord's prayer is all about the Father, *"After this manner therefore pray ye: Our Father which art in heaven, Hallowed be thy name. Thy kingdom come, Thy will be done in earth, as it is in heaven."* Matthew 6:9-10. The key to answered prayer is seeing the Father. *"…that whatsoever ye shall ask of the Father in my name, he may give it you."* John 15:16. Therefore, God is restoring the Father's heart back into the body of Christ. He is giving us back a great gift that has been lost for centuries. He is bringing us back into full health and strength in the leadership of the apostolic father. Just as an Elijah anointing was on the forerunner of the first coming of Christ, the same anointing will fall on forerunners of the second coming of Christ. As it was said of John the Baptist it will be said on the present prophetic generation. *"And he shall go before him in the spirit and power of Elias, to turn the hearts of the fathers to the children, and the disobedient to the wisdom of the just; to make ready a people prepared for the Lord."* Luke 1:17.

The Holy Spirit is raising up a troop of apostolic fathers who will be anointed to mentor and raise up sons and daughters who will be known as the Elisha generation that ushers in "The Day of the Lord". "The Day of the Lord" is the time of final judgments, final revival, and final harvest. At present, young pastors are running after church models, mainly the mega churches, to find success in church growth. This is about to change, the Holy Spirit is raising up a generation of sons and daughters who will pursue apostolic fathers. As I write, this supernatural shift is happening. So be it!

In the New Testament church, the apostle brought government and strategy for world missions, mobilized the army of God as a military commander and was the master builder of relations. His heart was to father and mentor sons and daughters. Listen to Paul's language in his letter to Timothy, *"Thou therefore, my son, be strong in the grace that is in Christ Jesus. And the things that thou hast heard of me among many witnesses, the same commit thou to faithful men, who shall be able to teach others also."* Then in II Timothy 1:2, he begins his salutation with these words, *"to Timothy, my dearly beloved son…"* An apostolic father does not build on church members; he builds on sons and daughters. He comes to bring affirmation to a prophetic generation that will defy the Anti-Christ and fulfill the exploits of the final overcomers at the end of the church age.

In defining the Elisha generation or the prophetic generation of sons and daughters who will usher in the Day of the Lord, I am going to define three terms that will describe their labor of ministry:

1. **Revival** – Just before the great outpouring of 1904 in Wales, the church was spiritually dead. The nation had drifted far from God, like the USA. Church attendance was poor and sin abounded on every side. In our nation, less than ten percent of the population attends church on a regular basis and sin does abound on every side. In Wales, the Spirit of God came suddenly and swept over the land. What was dead became alive and history reports that the churches were so crowded that the multitudes were unable to get in. In five weeks 20,000 were added to the local churches. Judges in several places were given white gloves because there were no cases. That is true revival. Let's cry out, God come and revive us again!

2. **Reformation** follows a spiritual awakening. There is a reconstruction or rearrangement that brings order. Reformation is a radical process involving correction, renovation, and recovery. A time of reformation is a season of revolutionary change. It is a season where the church is back into right order and structure, or restored into original pattern, purity and power. In this state of light and salt, she will gather

the multitudes and confront the evil in a nation.

3. **Revolution** (Webster's) means to bring about a very great change, an overthrow of government or social system, or a complete radical change. The good news: God is coming to the church not just with manifestations but with an anointing of radical activism to turn the world upside right… to overthrow our immoral, unjust social and political system.

In the late 1980's Frank Peritti prophesied the Elisha generation. *"These are the days when I will trouble the enemy through you. Different days that you have never know…I am going to require sacrifice of you…It takes people who lay down their lives for revolution to be birthed. I am going to require a sacrifice of your sons and daughters, says the Lord. And I am going to shake everything that can be shaken…once more I will shake the heavens and earth, the sea and the dry land and I will shake all nations. And the desire of the nations shall come and I will fill this house with my glory, says the Lord of Hosts. But there is going to be a revolution….The Lord says, There are churches that will be command posts for revolution and to these command posts I would say I am going to bring a revolution…I am going to bring a radical change that will transform whole regions…"* In Jesus name regions will be transformed. *I am going to bring the 18, 19, 20, 21 year olds and they will mentor the younger generation below them. High schoolers will mentor the generation under them. It will be a soon day, when there will be as many youth as adults in these command posts for revolution. Thus saith the Lord, I will move and I will not pass you by I will put the gift of evangelism in the youth of these churches...souls and souls will be saved. They will invade the High School campuses and the universities of their cities and the Lord says....get ready...get ready...get ready...for it begins today."*

The message of the arising forerunner generation is repentance. John the Baptist is our example. *"In those days came John the Baptist, preaching in the wilderness of Judaea, And saying, Repent ye: for the kingdom of heaven is at hand. For this is he that was spoken of by the prophet Esaias, saying, The voice of one crying in the wilderness, Prepare ye the way of the Lord, make his paths straight."* Matthew 3:1-3. On July 4, 2004, I had an encounter with the Holy Spirit. Mary, my wife, was attending a church picnic. I came home early and was not really seeking the Lord. Then, suddenly, God moved on me. In His presence, I began to weep and He began to speak and shared the following four thoughts with me that have set direction in my ministry:

1. "I am going to use you in spite of your sins and short comings."

2. "I am going to separate you from all that is carnal, seasonal and secular."

3. "I am going to break you into a thousand pieces and pour you out on the body of Christ." Little did I know that my oldest daughter would take her life four years later. Out of that nightmare, God has broken me into a thousand pieces and poured me out on the Body to bring hope and comfort to those around me. What Satan meant for my destruction, God Himself has turned for edification.

4. "I am going to baptize you with fire and give you the message of repentance to the body of Christ." Too many of our pulpits have forgotten the message of repentance and are preaching a gospel of convenience and easy believisms. The seeker-centered message is not the heartbeat of the cross; the message of inspiration and how to have the best life is not the centrality of true kingdom preaching. We must return to the message of the New Testament, "Repent ye, for the kingdom of Heaven is at hand."

Repentance means a change of mind, doing a 180° in someone's direction or life style. "It will take a radical church to reach a radical generation." (Bethany Conference.) "Radical" means going back to our roots, back to the power and purposes of the early church. By the way, what was wrong for the early church is wrong for the last church. What was right for the first church is right for the last church. *"Jesus Christ the same yesterday, today and forever."* Hebrews 13:8. Repentance was the message of our King, the true life changer: *"The people which sat in darkness saw great light; and to them which sat in the region and shadow of death light is sprung up. From that time Jesus began to preach, and to say, Repent: for the kingdom of heaven is at hand."* Matthew 4:16-17.

So the great good news is that presently God is raising up forerunners with a prophetic voice to bring repentance, accountability and order in to the Body. The Holy Spirit is not coming to disorder but to a generation of young people under apostolic authority and accountability. The shakers and movers of this generation will be in the spirit of the first church, *"And when the day of Pentecost was fully come, they were all with one accord in one place. And suddenly there came a sound from heaven as of a rushing mighty wind, and it filled all the house where they were sitting. And there appeared unto them cloven tongues like as of fire, and it sat upon each of them."* Acts 2:1-3. They were all filled with the wind and fire of the Holy Spirit and turned the whole world upside down. So be it.

In closing, the prophet Mike Bickles has God's heart and vision for our sons and daughters, "The Book of Revelation describes the main theme is Jesus' return to earth to rule all nations. Evil governments will resist this. His end-time battle plan is to physically destroy all the evil governments on earth by releasing His judgments on them during the Great Tribulation as described in Revelation 6-19. As the book of Acts describes the power of the Holy Spirit that was released through the early church, so the book of Revelation describes the power of the Holy Spirit that will be released through the end-time church.

I refer to Revelation as the "End-Time Book of Acts." It is a "canonized prayer manual" that informs us of the ways in which Jesus will manifest His power. As Moses released God's judgments on Pharaoh by prayer (Exodus 7-12), so the church will release the Great Tribulation judgments on the Anti-Christ by prayer. The miracles and judgments in Exodus and Acts will be multiplied and released worldwide through prayer. The greatest demonstrations of power in history will be openly manifest by Jesus and Satan. Revelation 12:9; 13:2. Revelation is Jesus' battle plan to allow the sin in man's heart to fully come to the surface and then to drive evil off the planet through the praying church. These judgment events do not happen to us as helpless victims of Satan but are released through us as participants with Jesus. Jesus' judgments are released to remove all that hinders love. He is at war to have his wedding." Mike Bickles, IHOP.

CHAPTER SEVEN

The Prophet To The Nation: Three Stages Of God's Judgments On A Nation

"Shall a trumpet be blown in the city, and the people not be afraid? shall there be evil in a city, and the LORD hath not done it? Surely the Lord GOD will do nothing, but he revealeth his secret unto his servants the prophets." Amos 3:6-7.

The First Stage: The Prophetic Voice

Here in the context of these scriptures there is a judgment that is coming on the land, and verse 6 gives God the credit – the punishment and the judgment comes from God. In verse 7, the prophet announces God's judgment. He will not carry out His judgment without a prophetic warning because God is long-suffering and merciful. Therefore, in His warning, He is calling out for repentance and reformation that He may measure out His forgiveness and mercy rather than His wrath and judgment. This is His ultimate desire. Then in verse 9, through the prophetic voice, He tells us that His message must be uttered far and wide. It is going to be a clear message, and it will go across all the land as He begins to warn the nation: *"Publish in the palaces at Ashdod, and in the palaces in the land of Egypt, and say assemble yourselves upon the mountains of Samaria, and behold the great tumults in the midst of thereof, and the oppressed in the midst thereof."* Amos 3:9.

The Greek word for "tumults" is "noise", and that denotes a state of confusion in the land. One meaning of this Hebrew word is that all justice and order has been overthrown by violence. That gives us a picture of America today. There is little justice left in the land as a whole. There are pockets of it left in the conservative areas of the South, but in the East, North, and parts of the West, there is hardly any justice left in the courtroom. Rather there is confusion and violence, and the criminal has become the hero.

There is a three-fold call of the church in this hour. The first function of the local church in the first stage of God's judgment is to be the prophetic voice. *"Cry aloud, spare not, lift up thy voice like a trumpet, and show My people their transgression, and the house of Jacob their sins."* Isaiah 58:1. Remind, people of their sin! Remind your land that God is alive! A nation that forgets God will perish. One of our main purposes as God's church is to remind our nation that He is alive, and that He is troubled by the violation of

His moral law and the injustice that is in the land. That is part of our calling in the prophetic. God said to the prophet Jeremiah, and I believe this is now His calling to the local church, *"Before thou camest forth out of the womb I sanctified thee and ordained thee a prophet unto the nations. This day I have set thee over the nations, over the kingdoms, to root out, to pull down and to destroy, and to throw down (that is judgment, to warn them, and to speak the judgments of God into the land), and then to build and to plant.* Jeremiah 1:5-10. The ultimate end of God's purpose in judgment is always restoration and redemption. Every local church is called to be a prophetic voice to her community and nation.

    The second function of the church in the first stage of judgment is to lead the way to national repentance. If we don't repent, the nation is not going to repent. There is a call for national repentance to which the church must respond. *"Blow ye the trumpet in Zion, and sound an alarm in My holy mountain: let all the inhabitants of the land tremble: for the day of the Lord cometh, for it is nigh at hand."* Joel 2:1. Zion is always a picture of the church, and the trumpet must be blown first in the church. The Day of the Lord in the prophet's mind is a day of awesome judgment and, of course, it is a picture of the final great tribulation judgments. Verse fifteen of the same chapter is a picture of repentance: *"Blow the trumpet in Zion, sanctify a fast, call a solemn assembly, gather the people, sanctify the congregation, assemble the elders, gather the children, and those that suck the breasts: let them say, spare thy people, O Lord and give not thine heritage to reproach, that the heathen should rule over them: wherefore should they say among the people, where is their God?"* Joel 2:15-17. Here we have a picture of repentance. Fasting always demonstrates a deep repentance towards God for the nation. We must repent for the sins of our nation.

The third function of the church in the first stages of God's judgment is that she is called to be an intercessor. *"And I sought for a man among them that should make up the hedge, and stand in the gap before Me for the land, that I should not destroy it: but I found none. Therefore have I poured out Mine indignation upon them; I have consumed them with the fire of My wrath: their own way have I recompensed upon their heads, said the Lord God"* Ezekiel 22:24, 30-31. We find here that the land of Israel was in a very poor moral condition, and God could not find an intercessor to throw up a hedge. The man who stands in the gap is a man who brings a nation back to God and away from sin. God said He could not find a man who would throw up a hedge, divert His wrath, and then, in the gap bring them back under His mercy of my forgiveness and Lordship. In other words, this kind of intercessor is not someone with lip service; it is someone who has a burden. As God moves on intercessors, there is a burden that comes with it. The burden is the anointing of the Holy Spirit that releases the inspired prayers of the Lord. As the burden comes upon local churches, it will be something that we live, eat, and sleep. It is not something that we will just meet for once a week, but it is something that will prevail all week. This kind of intercession will stay God's judgment and bring redemption to a nation.

James describes that kind of intercessor: *"...The effectual fervent prayer of a righteous man availeth much."* James 5:16. The man who has the burden, will sees the holiness of God. He sees how God's holiness has been transgressed by a nation, and he sees the wrath of God coming on a nation because God must balance the scales. Seeing a nation near desolation, the intercessor will make fervent supplication to God. When Moses went up Mt. Sinai, he saw God. He saw God's holiness. When he came down he saw sin. Often we must first see the holiness of God before we can see the sin of a nation and have a burden. The word "fervent" implies heat; there is heat in that prayer. The whole person, spirit, soul and body are in the spirit of prayer. This is the kind of intercessor God is speaking about. Another translation renders it this way: *"An upright man's prayer, when it keeps at work, is very powerful."* There is that continuous persistency of taking God's burden and speaking God's word across the land. Still another translation says: *"The earnest prayer of a righteous man makes tremendous power available. It is dynamic in its working."* (Amplified Bible) Later, I will address God's last call for intercessors.

The Second Stage of Judgment on a Nation: The Breaking of the Staff of Bread.

I have just described our three functions in the first stage of God's judgments. Now, if the church has only partial repentance, if the church moves with lip-service in intercession, and if she does not sound the prophetic voice like a trumpet, then the second stage begins. I believe that we are now in the second stage of God's judgment on America. I believe we have not rent our hearts; we have not yet paid the price to be God's prophetic voice and the intercessor. Therefore in this very hour, God is breaking the staff of bread across the nation. The breaking of the staff of bread is when food is being removed from the land, and people are actually beginning to hunger because there is no provision.

There are three basic biblical principles to look at as God begins to break the staff of bread. Understand that God is the sustainer of life. *"These wait upon Thee; that Thou mayest give them their meat in due season. That Thou givest them they gather: Thou openest Thine hand, they are filled with good. Thou hidest Thy face, they are troubled: Thou takest away their breath, they die, and return to dust."* Psalms 104:27-29. God rules in the kingdom of nature. The devil cannot devastate a land unless God gives permission. God is the creator; He is the sustainer of His creation. God is the source of all provision. When He removes His favor, His creation dies. This is expressed through the judgments of drought, floods, and famine.

Secondly, in understanding the breaking of the staff of bread, provisions are based on divine laws being satisfied. Leviticus shows us this principle: *"If ye walk in My statutes, and keep My commandments, and do them, then I will give you rain in due season, and the land shall yield her increase, and the trees of the field shall yield their fruit. And your threshing shall reach unto the vintage, and the vintage shall reach unto the sowing time: and ye shall eat your bread to the full, and dwell in your land safely."*

God will use violent weather conditions as He breaks the staff of bread (food supply). As I read through the prophets, I began to see this. No one ever taught this to me, nor did I read a book or hear a tape, but as I read the prophets this was revealed to me. *"The word of the Lord that came to Jeremiah concerning the dearth. Judah mourneth, and the gates thereof languish; they are black unto the ground; and the cry of Jerusalem is gone up. And their nobles have sent their little ones to the waters: they came to the pits and found no water; they returned with their vessels empty; they were ashamed and confounded, and covered their heads. Because the ground is chapt (cracked, parched), for there was no rain in the earth, the plowmen were ashamed, they cover their heads. Yea, the hind also calved in the field, and forsook it, because there was not grass. And the wild asses did stand in the high places, they snuffed the wind like dragons; their eyes did fail, because there was no grass. O Lord, though our iniquities testify against us, do Thou it for Thy name's sake: for our backslidings are many; we have sinned against Thee."* Jeremiah 14:1-7. The terrible weather conditions in our land are a part of the breaking of the staff of bread.

The United States is undergoing a nationwide drought, producing a crisis that some scientists believe will have greater consequences than rising sea levels. The devastating brush fires in Southern California are one side effect of this continuing drought. "The Deep South is also gripped by a prolonged drought, endangering the water supply for the 4.4 million residents of the Atlanta mega-metro area. The mighty Great Lakes are also shrinking, threatening shipping commerce due to historically low water levels. The Florida Everglades are being affected by Florida's continuing water emergency. This drought is having a deep and lasting effect on the choices regarding where we will want to live in the future. The crisis has been growing slowly, but it is finally getting attention in the national spotlight." *The Sperling Drought Index.*

"On April 28, 2011, a devastating drought intensified across Texas for over a week, with high winds and heat causing "massive crop losses." The latest report from a consortium of national climate experts said "the drought worsened along the Texas border with Oklahoma, as well as in western, central and southern Texas. Ranchers were struggling to feed and water cattle, and wheat farmers were left to watch their crops shrivel into the dusty soil. There was a slight alleviation of drought in central and eastern Oklahoma as more than seven inches of rain fell during the past week," *The Drought Monitor.* "But for farmers farther south, there was no relief in sight. Forecasters predicted that for May 3 through 7, the odds favor warmer-than-normal weather across the Southwest and South and into the Southeast and along the Gulf Coast." *Stated in Reuters* by Carey Gillam.

The value of water is starting to become apparent in America. Over the past three years a drought has affected large swaths of the country, and conflicts over water usage may become commonplace in the future, climatologists say. "Our focus is oil, but the critical need for water is going to make water the most significant natural resource that we're going to have to worry about in the future," says Larry Fillmer, executive director of the Natural Resources Management & Development Institute at Auburn University in Alabama. At least 36 states expect to face water shortages within the next five years, according to a report from the U.S. Government Accountability Office. According to the National Drought Mitigation Center, several regions in particular have been hit hard: the Southeast, Southwest, and the West.

According to the U.S. Geological survey, "the current drought in the West of North America is the worst that occurred in the last five hundred years with the water levels at close to half of the drought in early thirties of the previous century."

"And I also have given you cleanness of teeth (no meat) in all your cities, and want of bread in all your places: yet have ye not returned unto Me, saith the Lord. And also I have withholden the rain from you, when there were yet three months into harvest: and I caused it to rain upon one city, and caused it not to rain upon another city: one piece was rained upon, and the piece whereupon it rained not withered. So two or three cities wandered unto one city, to drink water; but they were not satisfied: yet have not returned unto Me, saith the Lord. I have smitten you with blasting and mildew: when your gardens and your vineyards and your fig trees and your olive trees in creased, the palmerworm devoured them:

yet have ye not returned unto Me saith the Lord." Amos 4:6-9. God was warning Israel with these weather conditions, but she would not listen. God desolated her. God is warning the church in America. We must hear the warning and blow the trumpet. We must intercede, and repent on behalf of the nation. If we do our job, the nation could be spared of destructive judgments.

There is a point in time as we move into the tribulation period when the rebellion of man will reach great heights. At this point, God has told us in Revelation 6, that there will be a famine of great magnitude that will sweep the world. This, in fact, might be happening now. I understand that even now, two-thirds of the world goes to bed hungry. We are moving into the season of the seals. I am not saying that the seal is broken; I am saying that the symptoms are here and that it may be near. *"And when he had opened the third seal, I heard the beasts say, A measure of wheat for a penny, and three measures of barley for a penny; and see thou hurt not the oil and the wine."* Revelation 6:5. We are the heartbeat of the world because the knowledge of God is here. If the breaking of the staff of bread begins here, worldwide famine will result. We have supplied much food to feed a big portion of the world. If this land loses the provision of God, it will be an awful thing throughout the world. Let us commit ourselves to function as a prophetic voice, to be a trumpet to the world, to be an intercessor, to stay in the spirit of repentance for our land, and to weep over the murders, the abortions, the injustices, and to be activist in every public arena.

The Third Stage of God's Judgment on a Nation: The Great Sword Judgments.

Let us now look at the third stage of God's judgment, which I pray fervently will never visit this nation. Ezekiel 14:21 tells us of the four sore acts of judgment: The famine or breaking of the staff of bread; noisome Beast (those beasts of the forest that usually come out after wars and devour the carcasses), the plagues or pestilence, and fourth, the sword of an enemy nation. *"Now this is what the Sovereign LORD says: How terrible it will be when all four of these dreadful punishments fall upon Jerusalem—war, famine, wild animals, and disease—destroying all her people and animals."* Ezekiel 14:21.

On September 11, 2000, referred to as 9-11, we experienced a small measure of the sword judgment against our land. I was fishing at the mouth of the Mississippi River when my cell phone rang and I was told the Twin Towers had fallen and thousands of innocent Americans had died. As I sat in utter shock, the Holy Spirit began to prophetically speak to my spirit; listed are four of those Rhemas:

- You were born for such a time as this.
- God said: Demonized terrorists are not going to have the last word, but I am going to have the last word on what has been done.
- This is the explosion heard around the world. This is the trigger for the final wars of the Middle East. They will not stop until Jesus sets His foot on the Mount of Olives and it splits in half.

- You have entered into the Day of the Lord: The time of final judgment, final wars, final revival and final harvest. So be it!

Ezekiel tells us of this great sword of judgment, the final judgment of God on one rebellious nation. Remember, Israel was warned over and over by droughts and crop losses and by the prophets. Finally, when she would not repent, God sent the sword and desolated her.

Now let us look at tribulation in Revelation, chapter 6. As the seals are breaking, we are in the beginning of the terrible and final judgments against the earth. As the first seal is broken, the Anti-Christ appears on the world scene. I believe we are in this season. *"And I saw, and behold a white horse: and he that sat on him had a bow; and a crown was given unto him: and he went forth conquering, and to conquer."* This is in reference to the lawless one, the Anti-Christ, who has come into power and is beginning to move, and establish his government. This is possibly already happening on the earth. Then the second seal is broken: *"And when he had opened the second seal, I heard the second beast say, Come and see. And three went out another horse that was red: and power was given to him that sat theron to take peace from the earth, and that they should kill one another and there was given unto him a great sword."* Revelation 6:3-4**.** There is a great sword judgment of God. Historians are telling us that across the world there has never been a time when peace has been so taken as it is now. Wars are going on in Central America, the Middle East, North Africa, the Far East, Afghanistan, Iraq, and Ireland. All over the world, man is at war. Again, we are in the season of the second seal. God is trying to get our attention.

In understanding God's judgment, we must understand His sovereignty in the rise of world powers. He is in control of the rise and fall of world powers; it is in His hands. Daniel 2 shows us the vision of the great image. *"Thou, O king sawest, and behold a great image. This great image, whose brightness was excellent, stood before thee; and the form thereof was terrible. This image's head was of fine gold, his breast and his arms of silver, his belly and his thighs of brass, his legs of iron, his feet part of iron and part of clay. Thou sawest till that a stone was cut out without hands, which smote the image upon his feet that were of iron and clay, and brake them to pieces."* Daniel 2:31-34. Here is God's prophetic word on the Gentile world-ruling empires that would rule until Jesus came and set up His kingdom. Later he gives interpretation, and says that the golden head was the Babylonian empire, which lasted until 538 B.C. The silver arms represented the Medo-Persian kingdom, which destroyed the Babylonian empire, and took over as a Gentile ruling empire from 528 to 331 B.C. The brass belly and thighs were the Grecian empire under Alexander the Great. The old Roman Empire represented by the legs of iron was ruling in Jesus' day (44 B.C. to 400 A.D.)

The feet of iron and clay represent the final Gentile world empire that will oppress Israel as a nation. This has been commonly referred to the future (revised) Roman Empire composed of ten nations (ten toes on the feet). The present European Common Market is possibly this final world empire which will rule under the Anti-Christ. This final world empire will be destroyed at our Lord's return as prophesied *"During the reigns of those kings, the God of heaven will set up a kingdom that will never be destroyed or conquered. It will crush all these kingdoms into nothingness, and it will stand forever."* Daniel 2:44. Gabriel and Michael are real, powerful, angelic beings that God is using to usher in these kingdoms. (Gabriel talking to Daniel) *"Then said he unto me, Fear not, Daniel: for from the first day that thou didst set thine heart to understand and to chasten thyself before thy God, thy words were heard, and I am come for thy words. But the prince of the kingdom of Persia withstood me, one and twenty days: but, low Michael, one of the chief princes, came to help me; and I remained with the kings of Persia."* Daniel 10:12.

The real battles are won in the heavenlies. Who won in the major wars of history depended on which ruling prince won in the heavenlies. God's angelic powers are involved in holding one satanic prince back and letting another one come over a territory. The prince of the kingdom of Medes and Persians is the prince that was fighting against Gabriel and Michael. Satan has fallen angels who try to carry out his will in government and to block God from carrying out His prophetic word. The prince over the Babylonian empire did not like to give way to the Medo-Persian prince. It took Michael and Gabriel hours to move that ruling prince out. Satan is trying to stop God from fulfilling His purposes in the

Gentile world empire. See the Heavenly warfare determining the rise and fall of a nation: *"Then said he knowest thou wherefore I come unto thee? And now will I return to fight with the prince of Persia: and when I am gone forth, lo, the prince of Grecia shall come."* Daniel 10:20. Gabriel and Michael were fighting off the Medo-Persian prince to allow the prince of Grecia to come in and give Alexander the Great his success and power.

When Iran and Iraq were in war, in the 1980's, I shared on the angelic powers participating to bring about the final result. No doubt there was a good angelic prince holding back one ruling principality to allow the one God wanted to take power. I predicated that Iran would be victorious because prophecy indicates that Iran is going to be in Russia's camp to invade the Middle East. Iran was victorious over Iraq and has become a partner in evil with Russia. By the way, Russia will resist the final Gentile world power being formed by the spirit of the Anti-Christ. In a later chapter, I will refer to prophecy that indicates Russia's removal as a world power along with her coalition which includes Iran.

Let us continue to see how God is raising up nations to fulfill His purposes. In Isaiah 45, God is talking to Cyrus, the king of Persia. This prophecy was given one hundred and fifty years before Cyrus was in power. God is calling the shots. *"Thus saith the Lord to His anointed, to Cyrus, whose right hand I have holden, to subdue nations before him; and I will loose the loins of kings, to open before him the two leaved gates; and the gates shall not be shut."* Isaiah 45:1. God is going to bring the Persian empire into power. God's purpose is revealed *"For Jacob My servant's sake, and Israel Mine elect, I have even called thee by thy name: I have surnamed thee, though thou hast not known Me."* Isaiah 45:4. For My people's sake I am calling you by your name to defeat the Babylonian empire that My people may be freed from the seventy years of captivity in fulfillment of God's word. There are many reasons why the Roman empire came into being and rose to historical prominence. She had the technology to build the roads to Jerusalem. She had the language to bring forth the Bible. This was all fulfillment of God's prophetic word in bringing forth the Messiah. God is in control. No nation comes into power unless it is somewhere in the prophetic planning of God. No nation falls unless God has allowed the angelic powers to bring it to pass.

Realize that our nation is under the judgments of God for the mass murder of babies, and the disregard for the moral law. See that the lion has come out of the thicket: Islam threatens war and take over; socialism rules our federal government; humanism corrupts our news media and public education; Jezebel runs Hollywood and is perverting the minds of our youth and millions of Americans. Understand that we are living in the Day of the Lord, God's time of final judgments, final revival, and final harvest. What should you do as an individual? How can you prepare for the end of the age? Simple, first and foremost keep your heart!

The heart is central in who you are and your ability to go through the gross darkness that has come and is increasing over the nations of the world. The fear of the Lord to hold God in awe; to reverence His name and His word. The fear of the Lord is to love righteousness and to hate sin. The fear of the Lord is *"to love God with all your heart, all your soul, and all your mind."* Matthew 22:32. The scripture teaches that the heart of man is central. Jesus said, *"Blessed are the pure in heart, for they shall see God."* Matthew 5:8.

Let us rejoice that our Father in Heaven has provided ransom for your heart. Jesus said, *"for God so loved the world (that's everyone) that He gave us His only begotten son (to ransom our hearts) that whosoever (the one) believeth in Him should not perish but have everlasting life."* John 3:16. Praise God, that the blood of Jesus was shed to ransom our hearts, to redeem us, to set us free from the power of sin, Satan, selfishness, and sickness. The Holy Spirit spoke through the prophet Ezekiel, *"A new heart will I give you I will move out the stony heart (old* lost *carnal heart)"* Ezekiel 36:26. In 1968, I received a heart transplant; God took out my stony selfish heart and gave me a new heart…my spirit was born again, regenerated. In a moment of time. Hebrews 8:10 happened, *"This covenant I will make with the house of Israel, I will put my laws into their minds (the engrafted word of God) and I will write my moral law in their hearts."*

One spring afternoon in 1968, the moral law was written in my heart, "thou shalt have no other god's before me; thou shall not take the name of the Lord God in vain; Remember the Sabbath day, keep it holy; don't kill; don't commit adultery; don't lie or bear false witness against your neighbor," and on and on the moral law was impregnated in my heart. In a moment of time, the moral law or the character of Christ was birthed in me by the Holy Spirit. Immediately, the cussing and taking God's name in vain left; the drunkenness and the adulteress heart was taken out of me; I started keeping the Sabbath holy…Sunday became a day of worship and celebration. On Sundays, I am with a congregation of believers encountering Jesus through the Holy Spirit, not chasing balls on a golf course or at a baseball or football field. Every born again believer reading these thoughts, be still and realize that God has given you a new heart. Therefore, your heart is not evil, it is good. You can follow your heart. Our struggles in walking out our new heart is in the battle in the mind. Our minds are messed up and have to be delivered of strongholds and renewed in the word of God.

Some thoughts from Mark Batterson's book *Primal:* "Your heart begins to break for the things that break the heart of God. And that is the heart of what it means to love God with all your heart. And when Jesus reveals the four primal elements of love, the heart comes first. I'm afraid that the Western church has tried to engage our culture mind-first instead of heart-first. But minds often remain closed to truth until hearts have been opened by compassion. There is certainly a place for logical, left brained explanations of faith. But compassion is the ultimate apologetic. There is no defense against it. Every year, fifteen million children die of starvation. When you break that number down, that is more than forty thousand children per day or nearly twenty-nine children every sixty seconds." *Primal* by Mark Batterson.

What is the heart? The heart is the spirit of man. We are a spirit that lives in a body and we have a mind. *"And the very God of peace sanctify you wholly; and I pray God your whole spirit and soul and body be preserved blameless unto the coming of our Lord Jesus Christ."* I Thessalonians 5:23. In 1968, my spirit got regenerated not my mind or body. The spirit of man is the place of conscience, intuition, revelation, and worship. As believers, we commune with the Holy Spirit with our hearts. Revelation comes like light into our hearts. The heart is where courage and conviction abide. Faith comes by hearing and hearing by the word of God. We hear with the third ear of our regenerated spirit, so faith is borne in our heart, not our heads. *"For with the heart man believes unto righteousness and with the mouth confession is made unto salvation."* Romans 10:10. Our relationship with Jesus under His Lordship is a heart not a head confession. A man's spirit is the place of dreams, visions, and callings. In our hearts, the Holy Spirit imparts a sense of divine destiny, God's plan and purpose for us in His Kingdom on earth. To the yielding believer, love is the language of our heart; that is we live to love God and to love people.

First and foremost, we must keep our hearts, because demonic powers are at war against the mind to assault the heart. *"For the weapons of our warfare are not carnal, but mighty through God to the pulling down of strong holds; Casting down imaginations, and every high thing that exalteth itself against the knowledge of God, and bringing into captivity every thought to the obedience of Christ."* II Corinthians 10:4-5. Strongholds are negative thought patterns that make inroads into our mind and put a bushel over our hearts. For example, a parent who is angry and harsh with a child will cause rejection thoughts to enter his mind. Eventually, a demonic stronghold is formed blocking the flow of the heart.

The devil's strategy is to make us so busy that we don't have time to take care of our hearts. One of my life messages is to take time out early in the morning to sit at the feet of Jesus, to be still and to see what He is saying. At daybreak, I sit at the feet of Jesus and receive grace, His strength to face the day. See the example of our Lord and Savior: *"But so much the more went there a fame abroad of him: and great multitudes came together to hear, and to be healed by him of their infirmities. And he withdrew himself into the wilderness, and prayed."* Luke 5:15-16**.** Jesus took time out to pray, to refuel, and to re-chart his course. Jesus said, *"I only do what I see my Father doing, whatever the Father does, the Son also does."* John 15:19. As believers, we must first and foremost take care of our hearts. We must be still and see what the Holy Spirit is saying and what He is doing. By morning, sit at the feet of Jesus and experience divine osmosis, absorb the grace of God to see the will, to be the will, and to do the will.

Also, remember that the devils strategy is to discourage and disappoint us until we forsake our heart. Or he comes to wound us so deeply through the setbacks and heartbreaks of life until we lose heart or simply give up in our service to the Lord. On December 11, 2008, my wife and I took a gut shot from the powers of darkness. Our oldest daughter, in her forty-fourth year, took her life in a depressed state. She was actually coming out of a deep state of guilt and depression when her mind apparently snapped under the voice of a spirit of suicide. In this tragedy, we came to two basic conclusions and decisions. First, that our daughter was a casualty of war. As a family, we had suffered at the hand of our enemy. Secondly, her death would not be in vain nor would it stop us in our ministry to father pastors and be a messenger of hope to the body. What Satan meant for our demise and destruction, God turned it for our edification. The Holy Spirit has deeply comforted us and out of this comfort, we are touching and encouraging thousands of believers. The devil's strategy has failed; we are hurting but healing; we are weeping but walking, and our weeping for the night has turned into joy by morning.

Therefore, in the midst of your heartbreak and setbacks, know that we are living in the season of the end of the age. We must first and foremost keep our hearts. *"My son, attend to my words; incline thine ear unto my sayings. Let them not depart from thine eyes; keep them in the midst of thine heart. For they are life unto those that find them, and health to all their flesh. Keep thy heart with all diligence; for out of it are the issues of life. Put away from thee a froward mouth, and perverse lips put far from thee."* Proverbs 4:20-24. This scripture admonishes us to let God's word penetrate deeply within our hearts and, above all else, to guard our hearts:

1. **The ear gates** – *"Put away from thee a froward mouth, and perverse lips put far from thee"* Proverbs 4:24.

Refuse negative talk. Flee discord that divides family, friends, and the body of Christ.

2. **The eye gates** – *"Let thine eyes look right on, and let thine eyelids look straight before thee."* Proverbs 4:25. What you behold, you become. Refuse to set any wicked scene before your eyes. Flee the seductive Jezebel media of Hollywood.

3. **Walk right** – *"Ponder the path of thy feet, and let all thy ways be established. Turn not to the right hand nor to the left: remove thy foot from evil."* Proverbs 4:26-27. Flee the close friendships of the opposite sex. Refuse to walk in places of darkness. Stay off the devil's grounds. So, first and foremost, guard your hearts, for out of your spirit man flows the issues of life: courage and conviction, vision, revelation and worship, the language of love, the joy and laughter of the Lord. All this flows from your inner man; refuse to compromise with the mindset of this present world system.

As we move into the end times, the final conflict with darkness, you must fight for your heart. Over my thirty-seven years of serving the Lord, I have observed many that quit fighting for their heart. Some lost their heart to addictions. Others lost their heart to the cares of this life. A few lost their hearts to illegal sexual affairs or an addiction to pornography. So many, too many, lost their hearts to an offense. You must fight for your heart: stay in the word; stay at the feet of Jesus; stay in a spirit of thanksgiving; live in a spirit of forgiveness, and stay committed to the local church or the place of your divine assignment.

In closing, seeing we are in the birth pangs of a new world order, you must connect with warriors who will fight for your heart. You must connect with covenant believers who are with you for better or for worse until death parts. *"And five of you shall chase an hundred, and an hundred of you shall put ten thousand to flight: and your enemies shall fall before you by the sword."* Leviticus 26:8. *"Again I say unto you, That if two of you shall agree on earth as touching any thing that they shall ask, it shall be done for them of my Father which is in heaven. For where two or three are gathered together in my name, there am I in the midst of them."* Matthew 18:19-20.

CHAPTER EIGHT

The Seven Sealed Book And The Season Of The Seals

"And I saw in the right hand of him that sat on the throne a book written within and on the backside, sealed with seven seals. And I saw a strong angel proclaiming with a loud voice, Who is worthy to open the book, and to loose the seals thereof? And no man in heaven, nor in earth, neither under the earth, was able to open the book, neither to look thereon. And I wept much, because no man was found worthy to open and to read the book, neither to look thereon. And one of the elders saith unto me, Weep not: behold, the Lion of the tribe of Judah, the Root of David, hath prevailed to open the book, and to loose the seven seals thereof."
Revelation 5:1-5.

The Revelator saw the seven-sealed book that contained the events of the future. In his heart, he knew that someone appointed by God must open the book and break the seven seals to release God's judgments against the Anti-Christ. He wept as he saw no qualified or God-anointed man who had the authority to release the power of the seven-sealed book. In His weeping, one of the twenty-four elder's declared to him that the Lion of Judah had prevailed to open the book. The seven-sealed book contained the events of the future and the title deed of the earth. The first Adam lost the title deed of the earth to the powers of darkness; the second Adam is taking back the title deed of the earth under the Kingdom of God. Therefore, the significance of the breaking of the seven seals is that God's time has come for the whole earth to be restored to its rightful heirs. *"The Spirit itself beareth witness with our spirit, that we are the children of God: And if children, then heirs; heirs of God, and joint-heirs with Christ; if so be that we suffer with him, that we may be also glorified together. For I reckon that the sufferings of this present time are not worthy to be compared with the glory which shall be revealed in us. For the earnest expectation of the creature waiteth for the manifestation of the sons of God."* Romans 8:16-19.

    Jesus Christ has paid the price of redemption and to restore all things unto Himself. It is His time to restore the earth unto the redeemed. As this begins to unfold, the heirs, the redeemed of the Lord, and the four beasts begin to worship the Lamb that had been slain: *And they sung a new song, saying, ...Saying with a loud voice, Worthy is the Lamb that was slain to receive power, and riches, and wisdom, and strength, and honour, and glory, and blessing. And every creature which is in heaven, and on the earth, and under the earth, and such as are in the sea, and all that are in them, heard I saying, Blessing, and honour, and glory, and power, be unto him that sitteth upon the throne, and unto the Lamb forever and ever."* Revelation 5:11-13.

Before I expound on the breaking of the seven seals, let us consider that we are moving into the season of the seals or into the season of their fulfillment. For example, between winter and spring there is a transition period. Consider the turbulent weather of an approaching spring. In the spring of 2011, there were the violent tornados that swept northern Alabama, killing over three hundred and causing hundreds of millions of dollars in property damage. In the same approaching spring and summer of 2011, a rising Mississippi River caused property damage of over three hundred million dollars just in the state of Louisiana.

I believe that we are in the transition period of the breaking of the seals and the release of God's awesome judgments on an Anti-Christ world system. Several years ago, I saw the tribulation period as a huge hurricane. Mid-tribulation is like the eye of a gigantic hurricane. From the eye, the destructive winds were released bringing desolation to our world as we know it. The further we move from the eye, the less violent the winds of the judgments. The tribulation period is set in time and history. In time, as we move toward the Great Tribulation, we begin to feel the gale winds of these destructive judgments. Our Lord Jesus exhorts us to discern the times we live in. *"The Pharisees also with the Sadducees came, and tempting desired him that he would shew them a sign from heaven. He answered and said unto them, When it is evening, ye say, It will be fair weather: for the sky is red. And in the morning, It will be foul weather today: for the sky is red and lowering. O ye hypocrites, ye can discern the face of the sky; but can ye not discern the signs of the times?"* Matthew 16:1-3. A spiritual man will discern the signs of the times. The Pharisees and Sadducees could not, they were religious people but not spiritual men, they could not discern the first coming of the Messiah or that He was with them. Neither will much of the religious or church world discern that His second coming is at hand nor that we are in the season of the breaking of the seven seals.

The following prophecy is two-fold in implication. It relates to A.D. 70 and also to a final desolation when the Anti-Christ sets up his rule in Jerusalem. *"Then let them which are in Judea flee to the mountains; and let them which are in the midst of it depart out; and let not them that are in the countries enter thereinto. For these be the days of vengeance, that all things which are written may be fulfilled. But woe unto them that are with child, and to them that give suck, in those days! For there shall be great distress in the land, and wrath upon this people. And they shall fall by the edge of the sword, and shall be led away captive into all nations: and Jerusalem shall be trodden down of the Gentiles, until the times of the Gentiles be fulfilled."* Luke 21:20-24.

The time of the Gentiles began with King Nebuchadnezzar of the Babylonian empire. This began the first world Gentile power and ended the world power of the Jewish nation. Ever since then, Jerusalem has been trodden down by the Gentiles. *"For I would not, brethren, that ye should be ignorant of this mystery, lest ye should be wise in your own conceits; that blindness in part is happened to Israel until the fullness the Gentiles be come in."* Romans 11:25. Here we see that same phrase, "the fullness of the Gentiles." This is now in the process of final fulfillment – it is happening right before our eyes. If you have a spiritual heart toward God, this will minister faith to you. Jerusalem had been under Gentile rule since the Babylonian empire. Now we see that this is slowly coming to an end. Israel has been restored as a nation. The prophet Isaiah saw it, *"I will gather thy seed from the east and the west and I will say to the north give up, and to the south keep not back."* Isaiah 43:5-6. In 1948, Israel was restored as a nation and is in place for God's final dealing with her as a nation.

Every Gentile world empire has persecuted the Jewish nation. In the fullness of the Gentiles, the final Gentile world power will arise and persecute Israel. The final world empire is the Anti-Christ government, where the ten kings will recognize him as world ruler. The season of the seals, is when this final world empire begins to come into power. We cannot stop it; it will happen in God's appointed hour. We are in the seasons of the seals. Let us discern the times we are living in as we begin to see this coming final Gentile world power which will persecute God's people.

With these thoughts in mind let us consider the four

riders of the Apocalypse who introduce the tribulation period. Apocalypse is an expectation of an imminent cataclysm which destroys the ruling power of evil and raises the righteous to life in a Messianic Dominion. (Webster's Dictionary)

The First Seal, the Rider on the White Horse. *"And I saw, and behold a white horse: and he that sat on him had a bow; and a crown was given unto him: and he went forth conquering, and to conquer."* Revelation 6:2. In the breaking of the first seal we see a counterfeit Christ being loosed on the world scene. We are in the season of the final forming of an evil world order. The seals will not be broken suddenly, but there will be a transition period, and this is what we are beginning to see.

The signs are:

1. The wealth and power structure of this Gentile world power is in the final stages of completion. The international bankers will be a part of that great system. Even now, they practically control the economy. Much of the church is in debt to the bankers. The Bible says that the borrower is a slave to the lender. A world-wide depression is seemingly on the scene, and then those who have wealth will accumulate more wealth.

2. The religious-political structure is almost in place. The ecumenical movement is the beginning of the formation of a one-world church which will come into power as prophesied in Revelation chapter 17: The religious-political

structure that will usher in the Anti-Christ will unite the ten kingdoms under a religious influence. At mid-tribulation, the Anti-Christ will destroy this religious system as he no longer needs it. The Trilateral Committee in America is part of that formation and is pushing for one world government. Some of the leaders in both political parties are trilateral members. The psychology for world peace dominates today's political thinking among the elitists.

The Second Seal, the Rider of the Red Horse. *"And when he had opened the second seal, I heard the second beast say, Come and see."* Revelation 6:3. The Great Sword is the release of the final wars on planet earth. "An unprecedented escalation of war has occurred in the twentieth century making it the bloodiest time in world history (over 100 million people killed). Since World War II, over 150 major wars have occurred with a death toll of over 25 million. Since the Berlin Wall fall (November 1989), conflicts have forced 50 million people from their homes world-wide. There were over 70 wars in 1995 (double from 1989)". Mike Bickles, IHOP.

During 2010 – 2011, it has seemed like the whole Middle East and parts of Africa were at war. We must be in the season of the second seal. I wrote earlier that 9-11 was the explosion heard around the world. On that dreadful day, the Holy Spirit said to me, "This is the beginning of the final wars of the Middle East. They will not stop until the Prince of Peace sets His feet on the Mount of Olives and it splits in half." (Read Zechariah 14:3-4). Ezekiel 38:1-6 is a prophetic description of one of the final great conflicts in which Russia and her allies will be destroyed, an event that will probably be called World War III. This event will be described in detail in a later chapter.

The final wars are moving toward Israel. Why? Because Christ Jesus is coming back to set up His millennium kingdom in Jerusalem. He will return through the Eastern Gate. The Anti-Christ knows this and will move his forces toward Jerusalem in an attempt to usurp God's authority. He will fail, because our Lord Jesus, in the brightness of His coming will destroy him and his armies with the sword that proceeds out of His mouth. (Read Revelation 19:19-21.)

Also, **we are in the season of the Black Horse, the Third Seal**. *"And when he had opened the third seal, I heard the third beast say, Come and see. And I beheld, and lo a black horse; and he that sat on him had a pair of balances in his hand. And I heard a voice in the midst of the four beasts say, A measure of wheat for a penny, and three measures of barley for a penny; and see thou hurt not the oil and the wine."* Revelation 6:5-6. One of the signs of the second coming of our Lord says in this scripture that food will be by measure, symbolizing scarcity. One measure was equal to one quart and that was a slave's daily ration. One penny usually bought eight measures, and here, one penny only buys one measure. Therefore, according to this prophecy, food will be eight times the cost it normally is.

In this country, we have had droughts in 1977, 1980, 1983 and more severe droughts in the past decade, 2000-2011. The hand of God is slowly breaking the staff of bread, warning the church and calling us to repentance. We are moving into a season of world-wide famine. "Nearly a billion people world-wide suffer from malnutrition. Over 25,000 people die every day world-wide from hunger related causes. Nearly 5 million die of starvation every year. Water shortages have reduced the global food supply by ten percent. Over 500 million people do not have enough drinking water. The numbers increase to two billion by 2025, thus, the greatest famine in world history." Mike Bickles, IHOP. Therefore, we are in the season of the breaking of the staff of bread of world-wide food collapse.

The Fourth Seal, the Rider of the Pale Horse. *"And I looked, and behold a pale horse: and his name that sat on him was Death, and Hell followed with him. And power was given unto them over the fourth part of the earth, to kill with sword, and with hunger, and with death, and with the beasts of the earth."* Revelation 6:8. This is further and more intense sword and famine judgments concluding the second and third seal.

The Fifth Seal, the Martyring of Believers. *"And when he had opened the fifth seal, I saw under the altar the souls of them that were slain for the word of God, and for the testimony which they held: And they cried with a loud voice, saying, How long, O Lord, holy and true, dost thou not judge and avenge our blood on them that dwell on the earth? And white robes were given unto every one of them; and it was said unto them, that they should rest yet for a little season, until their fellow servants also and their brethren, that should* *be killed as they were, should be fulfilled."* Revelation 6:9-11.

We are in the season of increasing hostility against the born-again church. More believers are being martyred in the past decade than in previous decades of this past century. As this seal is broken, there are two factors that will bring the one-world, Anti-Christ government against the body of Christ. First, there will be multitudes being saved in the darkness of the tribulation. And as we begin to pull people out of religion and the Anti-Christ system, the enemy will become angry and will persecute the true believers. Secondly, God's anointed will openly challenge this harlot system. Then the great whore will begin to have the church killed through Anti-Christ governments and power politics. *"And upon her forehead was a name written, mystery, Babylon the Great, the Mother of harlots and abominations of the earth. And I saw the woman drunken with the blood of the saints, and with the blood of the martyrs of Jesus: and when I saw her, I wondered with great admiration."* Revelation 17:5-6.

There are two marks during the tribulation period, *"And the LORD said unto him, Go through the midst of the city, through the midst of Jerusalem, and set a mark upon the foreheads of the men that sigh and that cry for all the abominations that be done in the midst thereof. And to the others he said in mine hearing, Go ye after him through the city, and smite: let not your eye spare, neither have ye pity."* Ezekiel 9:4-5. God's angelic seal protects the believer from the end time judgments of God. The other seal is for the Anti-Christ followers and will protect them from persecution and death. (Read Revelation 13:15-18.)

Also, in the midst of world-wide food collapse, God says that He will provide for His own. *"The LORD knoweth the days of the upright: and their inheritance shall be forever. They shall not be ashamed in the evil time: and in the days of famine they shall be satisfied. But the wicked shall perish, and the enemies of the LORD shall be as the fat of lambs: they shall consume; into smoke shall they consume away. I have been young, and now am old; yet have I not seen the righteous forsaken, nor his seed begging bread."* Psalms 37:18-20, 25. Whatever part of the church is here in the tribulation may be persecuted and killed by the Anti-Christ but we will not be taken out by starvation or any of God's judgments. We will be protected, even as the Israelites were in the land of Goshen.

The Sixth Seal, releases three significant events. *"And I beheld when he had opened the sixth seal, and, lo, there was a great earthquake; and the sun became black as sackcloth of hair, and the moon became as blood; And the stars of heaven fell unto the earth, even as a fig tree casteth her untimely figs, when she is shaken of a mighty wind. And the heaven departed as a scroll when it is rolled together; and every mountain and island were moved out of their places. And the kings of the earth, and the great men, and the rich men, and the chief captains, and the mighty men, and every bondman, and every free man, hid themselves in the dens and in the rocks of the mountains; And said to the mountains and rocks, Fall on us, and hide us from the face of him that sitteth on the throne, and from the wrath of the Lamb: For the great* *day of his wrath is come; and who shall be able to stand?"* Revelation 6:12-17.

First, there is a great earthquake. A major judgment is being released. Before going further, let me express the basic purpose of this Great Tribulation Period. "The main theme of Revelation is our Lord's return to earth to rule all nations. Evil governments will resist this. His end time battle plan is to physically destroy all the evil governments on earth by releasing His judgments on them during the Great Tribulation as described in Revelation chapters 6-19. Revelation is Jesus' battle plan to allow the sin and rebellion in man's heart to fully surface and then to drive evil off the planet through the prayers of the church. He is at war to have His wedding." Mike Bickles, IHOP. Prophet Bickles' overview and insight of Revelation bears witness with my spirit. God is always at war with evil and in the final seven years of earth as we know it, God fully releases His wrath against the evil of Satan and all his rule in planet earth.

The second significant event is the Revelation that the great day of His wrath has come. *"For the great day of his wrath is come; and who shall be able to stand?"* Revelation 6:17. The fierce wrath of God will be poured out against every follower and supporter of the Beast; the Anti-Christ, the human personification of Satan.

The third possible significant event of the sixth seal is rapture, the translation of the church into heaven or the first resurrection. We will see the possibility of this glorious event later in my writings during the blowing of the seventh trumpet.

Paul writing to the church at Thessalonica describes this great event. *"For this we say unto you by the word of the Lord, that we which are alive and remain unto the coming of the Lord shall not prevent them which are asleep. For the Lord himself shall descend from heaven with a shout, with the voice of the archangel, and with the trump of God: and the dead in Christ shall rise first: Then we which are alive and remain shall be caught up together with them in the clouds, to meet the Lord in the air: and so shall we ever be with the Lord."* I Thessalonians 4:15-17. The biblical support of the possible rapture after the sixth seal is the language of Matthew 24:29-31, the same as Revelation 6:12-17. *"Immediately after the tribulation of those days shall the sun be darkened, and the moon shall not give her light, and the stars shall fall from heaven, and the powers of the heavens shall be shaken: And then shall appear the sign of the Son of man in heaven: and then shall all the tribes of the earth mourn, and they shall see the Son of man coming in the clouds of heaven with power and great glory. And he shall send his angels with a great sound of a trumpet, and they shall gather together his elect from the four winds, from one end of heaven to the other."* Matthew 24:29-31.

The Seventh Seal, releases the Seven Trumpet Judgments. *"And when he had opened the seventh seal, there was silence in heaven about the space of half an hour. And I saw the seven angels which stood before God; and to them were given seven trumpets. And another angel came and stood at the altar, having a golden censer; and there was given unto* *him much incense, that he should offer it with the prayers of all saints upon the golden altar which was before the throne."* Revelation 8:1-3. This is the day of God's great wrath on the Anti-Christ and a world in total rebellion. "The trumpet judgments are supernatural acts of God through nature (first four trumpets) and through the release of demons (fifth and sixth trumpet) to destroy the resources of Anti-Christ." Mike Bickles, IHOP.

Realizing that we are in the season of the seals or in the gale winds of the Great Tribulation Period, it should provoke several responses from the heart of the body of Christ:

1. United Prayer and Fasting as we prepare for the return of the bridegroom.

2. Allow the Holy Spirit to prepare us for the final conflict with Anti-Christ; God is at war with evil. He invites us to join Him to stand against all evil.

3. Stay connected to our individual assignment to the local body and connect with warriors.

4. Separate from all that secular, sensual, and carnal.

5. The signs of the approaching Great Tribulation are the dinner bell for harvest. When the judgments of God are in the earth, the inhabitants of the earth learn righteousness. Let's prepare and lay down our lives for world evangelism.

6. Acknowledge the apostolic fathers who will mobilize

the church for the final harvest and raise up a prophetic generation of sons and daughters …the manchild!

7. Live in expectation that the glory of God will fill every local church that is under apostolic authority. *"Arise, shine; for thy light is come, and the glory of the LORD is risen upon thee. For, behold, the darkness shall cover the earth, and gross darkness the people: but the LORD shall arise upon thee, and his glory shall be seen upon thee. And the Gentiles shall come to thy light, and kings to the brightness of thy rising."* Isaiah 60:1-3.

Chapter Nine

Israel And The Final Wars Of The Middle East

In the fall of 1958, I was attending college at the University of Southwestern, Lafayette, Louisiana. While attending, I joined the Air Force Reserve Officers Training Corp. Captain Stewart of the Air Force was the commander directly over our squad. During one classroom session, out of nowhere, he shared with us to keep our eyes on Israel; it would be the hot spot for future wars. Even though at the time I was not a believer, his thought impressed me and stayed in my memory. Listen to the prophet Zechariah, *"Behold, I will make Jerusalem a cup of trembling unto all the people round about, when they shall be in the siege both against Judah and against Jerusalem. And in that day will I make Jerusalem a burdensome stone for all people: all that burden themselves with it shall be cut in pieces, though all the people of the earth be gathered together against it."* Zechariah 12:2-3. Notice the language of the scripture, "I will make Jerusalem a trembling cup...and in that day will I make Jerusalem a burdensome or a heavy stone..." The conflict between Islam and the ancient Jewish people has become a burden or a heavy stone to all the major world powers of the nations. The Presidents of the United States and their diplomats have spent months and years of peace negotiations to prevent major wars. But even in this day and hour, May of 2011, there is no peace. Jerusalem remains the cup of trembling for the whole Middle East region. The surrounding Islam countries, with the supporting nations such as Russia and China, ought to beware of who is supporting the small nation of Israel. Again, let's listen to the prophet Zechariah, *"In that day shall the LORD defend the inhabitants of Jerusalem; and he that is feeble among them at that day shall be as David; and the house of David shall be as God, as the angel of the LORD before them. And it shall come to pass in that day, that I will seek to destroy all the nations that come against Jerusalem."* Zechariah 12:8-9. By the way, I believe we are living in the season of that day.

Then on that dreadful day of 9-11-2000, the terrorists struck down the Twin Towers, murdering over three thousand innocent Americans. As I sat stunned and shocked, the Holy Spirit began to quicken words to me in regards to this prophetic event. Note: I have referred to this in other parts of this writing but I must address it again in detail.

The first Rhema word was, **"You were born for such a time as this!"** The Holy Spirit has raised me up as a prophetic voice to blow the trumpet and warn the local churches to prepare for the final judgments of God, even the Great Tribulation.

The second Rhema word was, **"We have moved into the Day of the Lord, the time of final rebellion."** The rise of the Anti-Christ and a Christ-hating, church-hating world system, the time of final judgments against the Anti-Christ system of our world order, and the time of final revival and final harvest will come. Again, the glory of God will visit the local churches that are united under apostolic authority. If you are in a local church not under apostolic authority leave and find one that is in divine order and unity.

The third Rhema word, God said, **"Demonized terrorists will not have the last word, I will have the last word."** God rules and reigns! Listen to the words of Paul writing to the church at Ephesus, *"All this energy issues from Christ: God raised him from death and set him on a throne in deep heaven, in charge of running the universe, everything from galaxies to governments, no name and no power exempt from his rule. And not just for the time being, but forever. He is in charge of it all, has the final word on everything and is at the center of all this."* Ephesians 1:20-21.

The fourth Rhema word, **"This is the explosion heard around the world."** This is the trigger for the final wars of the Middle East. The wars in Afghanistan and Iraq were the beginning of those final wars in the Middle East. In this time period of world history, they will not stop until the fulfillment of prophecy declared by Zechariah the prophet: *"Behold, the day of the LORD cometh, and thy spoil shall be divided in the midst of thee. For I will gather all nations against Jerusalem to battle; and the city shall be taken, and the houses rifled,* and the women ravished; and half of the city shall go forth into captivity, and the residue of the people shall not be cut off from the city. Then shall the LORD go forth, and fight against those nations, as when he fought in the day of battle. And his feet shall stand in that day upon the mount of Olives, which is before Jerusalem on the east, and the mount of Olives shall cleave in the midst thereof toward the east and toward the west, and there shall be a very great valley; and half of the mountain shall remove toward the north, and half of it toward the south."* Zechariah 14:1-4. What a glorious day that will be when our Lord Jesus returns to Jerusalem to end the final wars of planet earth and bring peace to mankind!

Let's consider some more Bible prophecy and world history that points to the final wars of the Middle East. In the gospel of Luke, our Lord Jesus is prophesying under a heavy burden, *"And when he was come near, he beheld the city, and wept over it, Saying, If thou hadst known, even thou, at least in this thy day, the things which belong unto thy peace! but now they are hid from thine eyes. For the days shall come upon thee, that thine enemies shall cast a trench about thee, and compass thee round, and keep thee in on every side, And shall lay thee even with the ground, and thy children within thee; and they shall not leave in thee one stone upon another; because thou knewest not the time of thy visitation."* Luke 19:41-44. In A.D. 70, this prophetic judgment was fulfilled. The Roman General Titus and his armies surrounded Jerusalem, cutting them off from food supply. Jerusalem went into famine and was leveled during this destructive siege. This was the beginning of the great dispersion prophesied by our Lord Jesus, *"In your patience possess ye your souls. And when ye shall see Jerusalem compassed with armies, then know that the desolation thereof is nigh. Then let them which are in Judaea flee to the mountains; and let them which are in the midst of it depart out; and let not them that are in the countries enter thereinto. For these be the days of vengeance, that all things which are written may be fulfilled."* Luke 21:19-22. This was judgment on the nation of Israel for rejecting her Messiah, the Lord Jesus. *"And they shall fall by the edge of the sword, and shall be led away captive into all nations: and Jerusalem shall be trodden down of the Gentiles, until the times of the Gentiles be fulfilled."* Luke 21:24. The Jews were to be dispersed until the emerging of the final Gentile world empire, United Europe.

Israel, God's old covenant people, has been dispersed for nineteen centuries. They have suffered persecution throughout the centuries. In the 1200's, the Jews were banished from Spain. In the 1600's, they were massacred by the Russians in the Ukraine. In the 1940's, Adolf Hitler and his diabolical cohorts murdered six million innocent Jews. Again, we see a fulfillment of a self proclaimed prophecy: Pilate pleaded for the life of Jesus, but the religious Jews demanded His crucifixion. Then, Pilate took the following action, *"When Pilate saw that he could prevail nothing, but that rather a tumult was made, he took water, and washed his hands before the multitude, saying, I am innocent of the blood of this just person: see ye to it. Then answered all the people, and said, His blood be on us, and on our children."* Matthew 27:24-25. So be it; the blood of the Lord Jesus Christ has been on the Jewish nation for over nineteen centuries. It is a miracle, that through all of the dispersion and persecution, the Jewish people have stayed intact and maintain their identity as a separate nation.

Since A.D. 70, fewer than one thousand Jews have lived in Israel and the Gentiles have occupied the land for over nineteen hundred years. However, the last sixty years, we have seen the regathering of the Jews to her motherland as promised by the Abrahamic covenant. *"And the LORD appeared unto Abram, and said, Unto thy seed will I give this land: and there builded he an altar unto the LORD, who appeared unto him"* Genesis 12:7. This is a covenant promise, *"I will give unto thy seed the land."* This means the land of Canaan, Israel the Holy land. Its boundaries are described in Number 34:1-29. President Obama is wrong in wanting Israel to give up her land to make a Palestine state reverting to boundaries recognized before the 1967 war. It is obvious, that he favors the Muslim world over the nation of Israel. God help the United States of America to stand with Israel in her sovereignty and her covenant Promised Land.

The prophets of old predicted the regathering of God's ancient covenant people. *"Fear not: for I am with thee: I will bring thy seed from the east, and gather thee from the west; I will say to the north, Give up; and to the south, Keep not back: bring my sons from far, and my daughters from the ends of the earth; Even every one that is called by my name: for I have created him for my glory, I have formed him; yea, I have made him."* Isaiah 43:5-7. *"And say unto them, Thus saith the Lord GOD; Behold, I will take the children of Israel from among the heathen, whither they be gone, and will gather them on every side, and bring them into their own land: And I will make them one nation in the land upon the mountains of Israel; and one king shall be king to them all: and they shall be no more two nations, neither shall they be divided into two kingdoms any more at all. The heathen shall know that I the LORD do sanctify Israel, when my sanctuary shall be in the midst of them for evermore."* Ezekiel 37:21-22, 28.

Glory to God; in the past six decades, we have been seeing these prophecies come to pass. On May 14, 1948, the Prime Minister of England said these words, "The state of Israel will be open to the immigration of Jews from all countries of their dispersion." The supernatural return of the Jews to their promise land legally. In the first eighteen months, 340,000 returned, one in every three minutes from over one hundred countries. Only four out of one hundred had any money at all. When their independence was announced 655,000 Jews occupied their land. In the next three years, over 600,000 more came home. By 1965, 2.2 million Jews resided in her borders. By 1977, 3,610,000 occupied the old promise land.

In 2011, the population of Israel was 7,695,000. Seventy-five percent are Jews and twenty percent are Arabs. God's word has and is being fulfilled in our lifetime. There is still much more to come. The prophet Ezekiel declared that

God would restore her and place a King over her. *"And say unto them, Thus saith the Lord GOD; Behold, I will take the children of Israel from among the heathen, whither they be gone, and will gather them on every side, and bring them into their own land: And I will make them one nation in the land upon the mountains of Israel; and one king shall be king to them all: and they shall be no more two nations, neither shall they be divided into two kingdoms any more at all."* Ezekiel 37:21-22. The Messiah over Israel will be restored in the seventieth prophetic week prophesied by Daniel. (Read Daniel 9:24-27.) The seventieth week is the final seven years of the church age or what is referred to as the "Great Tribulation Period." Two main purposes of the tribulation period:

    1. **One purpose is God's judgments against the Anti-Christ and his world system.** He, the Lord, will eradicate evil from the planet earth through the release of His awesome judgments and take in a great harvest through the end-time body of committed believers. "The main theme of Revelation is Jesus' return to earth to rule all nations. Evil or Anti-Christ governments will resist this, but our Lord's end-time battle plan will physically destroy all evil governments on earth by releasing His judgments described in Revelation chapters 6-19. He will utterly drive out evil of the planet through the praying church. He is at war to have His wedding." Mike Bickles, IHOP.

    2. **The second purpose of Daniel's seventieth week or the last seven years of the church age is to deal with Israel one last time revealed Jesus as Messiah.** *"And it shall come*

to pass in that day, that I will seek to destroy all the nations that come against Jerusalem. And I will pour upon the house of David, and upon the inhabitants of Jerusalem, the spirit of grace and of supplications: and they shall look upon me whom they have pierced, and they shall mourn for him, as one mourneth for his only son, and shall be in bitterness for him, as one that is in bitterness for his firstborn." Zechariah 12:9-10.

The great image described by Daniel the prophet has five parts. (Read Daniel 2:31-45.) Each part, according to historians and theologians, represents a Gentile world power that persecutes the Jewish nation. Four of these empires have already come to pass:

- The golden head depicted the Babylonian Empire, 625 to 536 B.C.

- The silver portion was the Persian Empire, 536 to– 330 B.C.

- The brass part was the Grecian Empire, 330 to 166 B.C.

- The iron part was the great Roman Empire, 63 BC to approximately 100 A.D.

The final part is the ten toes, part iron and part clay. The ten toes depict ten kings. Most of us believe that this has come into its form at present. There are ten major nations that represent or occupy the territory of the old Roman Empire. They have formed the European Common Market which is becoming a major economic power through-out the world. This is probably going to be the final world Gentile ruling power that will serve the person of Anti-Christ as its leader. Through the European Common Market, Anti-Christ would have the economic means to control the resources of the world markets. We shall see what unfolds in this region during this decade.

There is some indication that the national leaders of Russia are not one-world government thinkers. They have not fallen into this demonic deception as the leaders of the United States seemed to have embraced. Therefore, Russia could be a hindrance to this Anti-Christ system which seems to be forming. Let's see what seems to be Russia in prophecy: *"And the word of the LORD came unto me, saying, Son of man, set thy face against Gog, the land of Magog, the chief prince of Meshech and Tubal, and prophesy against him, And say, Thus saith the Lord GOD; Behold, I am against thee, O Gog, the chief prince of Meshech and Tubal: And I will turn thee back, and put hooks into thy jaws, and I will bring thee forth, and all thine army, horses and horsemen, all of them clothed with all sorts of armour, even a great company with bucklers and shields, all of them handling swords: Persia, Ethiopia, and Libya with them; all of them with shield and helmet: Gomer, and all his bands; the house of Togarmah of the north quarters, and all his bands: and many people with thee."* **Ezekiel 38:1-6.** According to historians, the land of Magog and the tribes of Meshech, Tubal, and Gog are located in the northern region know as Russia. One of Russia's allies is Persia, known today as Iran and hell-bent to annihilate Israel as a nation. Libya and Ethiopia would include the twelve nations of Africa, North of Egypt. Seven of these are pro-Russian and anti-Israel.

The coming together of these allies is described, *"Therefore, son of man, prophesy and say unto Gog, Thus saith the Lord GOD; In that day when my people of Israel dwelleth safely, shalt thou not know it? And thou shalt come from thy place out of the north parts, thou, and many people with thee, all of them riding upon horses, a great company, and a mighty army: And thou shalt come up against my people of Israel, as a cloud to cover the land; it shall be in the latter days, and I will bring thee against my land, that the heathen may know me, when I shall be sanctified in thee, O Gog, before their eyes."* Ezekiel 38:14-16. This was almost fulfilled in the 1973 war when Egypt and Syria were invading Israel to destroy her as a nation. It was called, the "War of Annihilation." On the Syrian front, an Israelite tank lieutenant was called to intercept that massive invasion and was outnumbered fifty-to-one. There, in a supernatural effort of fighting almost single-handedly, the lieutenant went from knoll to knoll, knocking out one Russian tank after another. Just as in the Old Testament, Syria was so overwhelmed at the power and velocity of these warriors of Israel that she fled in retreat and headed back to Damascus. This, again, is a fulfillment of prophecy that *"in that day shall the Lord defend the inhabitants of Jerusalem…the feeble among them in that day shall be as David and an angel of the Lord was before them."* Zechariah 12:8.

There is no doubt in my mind that in that conflict between the north and the south, the angel of the Lord was before them. To the south, the Egyptian front advanced and was surprised that they could only reach that far, and no further. This gave time for the Israeli army to mobilize. By the way, between that line and Tel Aviv, there were only ninety battered tanks to stop them. They could have gone right through. But in that moment of surprise and fear, the Israeli armies trapped them and pushed them back. At that point Russia contacted the United States and warned that if Israel did not stop, she would invade. Russia loaded her cargo planes with paratroopers, prepared cruisers and battleships, and geared for what looked like World War III. The Israeli leadership heeded the appeals of the United States government and prolonged her invasion of Egypt and Syria. The prophecy of Russia's invasion was close to being fulfilled. But God's timing was not yet.

Now, and again, we are seeing war signals on the Syrian front. The scene is being set. Israel plans to go all-out the next time. What will happen when this begins to take place? Then in Ezekiel 39, *"Therefore, thou son of man, prophesy against Gog, and say, Thus saith the Lord God; Behold I am against thee, O Gog, the chief prince of Meshech and Tubal; And I will turn thee back, and leave but the sixth part of thee, and will cause thee to come up from the north parts, and will bring thee upon the mountains of Israel: And I will smite thy bow out of they left hand, and will cause thine arrows to fall out of thy bands, and the people that is with thee: I will give thee unto the ravenous birds of every sort, and to the beasts of the field to be devoured. Thou shalt fall upon the open field: for I have spoken it, saith the Lord God. And I will send a fire on Magog, and among them that dwell carelessly in the isles: and they shall know that I am the Lord. So will I make My holy name known in the midst of My people Israel; and I will not let them pollute My holy name any more: and the heathen shall know that I am the Lord, the Holy One in Israel."* Ezekiel 39:1-7. It goes on to say that for seven years they will bury the armies of Russia on the plains of Megedda. When this takes place, there will be no foe to the European Common Market. There will be no hindrance to the final world empire. In that hour, the power of the Anti-Christ will come into being, creating the final Gentile world-ruling empire. Then we will see the makings of a world in total rebellion. For that hour, God is preparing His church and trying to alert the world of His impending judgment.

When these things begin to happen, our Lord Jesus said, *"...look up, for your redemption draweth nigh,"* Luke 21:28. And we thank God for it. This is the church's time to get busy to fulfill the Lord's purpose and to bring in the great harvest. As these things take place, many will come to the church for answers. We must be ready to give them God's answer – Jesus Christ crucified, Jesus Christ sanctifier, Jesus Christ, the coming Lord and judge of the world. We look forward to that hour and we rejoice in this hour.

Chapter Ten

The Seventieth Week: The Day Of The Lord, The Final Seven Years

The Old Testament prophets spoke of the Day of the Lord as time set in world history where God will bring final judgments on evil. Isaiah the prophet saw it, *"Howl ye; for the day of the LORD is at hand; it shall come as a destruction from the Almighty."* Isaiah 13:6. The Day of the Lord is a day of darkness, God's wrath and great tribulation: *"Woe unto you that desire the day of the LORD! To what end is it for you? The day of the LORD is darkness, and not light."* Amos 5:18. The Day of the Lord is day of the final wars of the Middle East: *"Behold, the day of the LORD cometh, and thy spoil shall be divided in the midst of thee. For I will gather all nations against Jerusalem to battle; and the city shall be taken, and the houses rifled, and the women ravished; and half of the city shall go forth into captivity, and the residue* of the people shall not be cut off from the city. Then shall the LORD go forth, and fight against those nations, as when he fought in the day of battle."* Zechariah 14:1-3. The Day of the Lord is the day of the return of the Lord Jesus to planet earth, *"And his feet shall stand in that day upon the mount of Olives, which is before Jerusalem on the east, and the mount of Olives shall cleave in the midst thereof toward the east and toward the west, and there shall be a very great valley; and half of the mountain shall remove toward the north, and half of it toward the south."* Zechariah 14:4. The Day of the Lord is the day God sets up the thousand-year reign of Jesus Christ as Lord and King over all the earth.

Again, Prophet Mike Bickles gives a simple explanation of the "Day of the Lord." *"And the LORD shall utter his voice before his army: for his camp is very great: for he is strong that executeth his word: for the day of the LORD is great and very terrible; and who can abide it?"* Joel 2:11. "The Day of the Lord refers to unusual events that will escalate dramatically in the three and a half years just before Jesus Christ returns. The two-fold nature of this time is seen in the great blessings it releases on those who call upon Jesus, and judgments on those who refuse Him. It will be a Great Day to those who call on Jesus' name because they will experience the greatest outpouring in world history. *"And it shall come to pass afterward, that I will pour out my spirit upon all flesh; and your sons and your daughters shall prophesy, your old men shall dream dreams, your young men shall see visions: And also upon the servants and upon the handmaids in those days will I pour out my spirit. And I will shew wonders in the heavens and in the earth, blood, and fire, and pillars of smoke."* Joel 2:28-32. In this great revival, the Holy Spirit will release the miracles seen in the book of Acts and Exodus, even greater than on a global scene. It will be a terrible day to the rebellious or the Anti-Christ followers. They will experience the most severe judgments of God during the last three and a half years of the seventieth week or in the Day of the Lord;" *"For then shall be great tribulation, such as was not since the beginning of the world to this time, no, nor ever shall be. And except those days should be shortened, there should no flesh be saved: but for the elect's sake those days shall be shortened."* Matthew 24:21-22. Mike Bickles, IHOP.

Referring to the scripture and the understanding shared; let me briefly define the Day of the Lord: It will be the season of the final wars of the Middle East, and God's final dealings with the nation of Israel. God will issue final judgments on Anti-Christ and the Anti-Christ nations, and the final great outpouring coupled with the greatest harvest of souls in world history. Jesus Christ will return as He takes down Anti-Christ, and then the thousand-year reign of Christ Jesus governing from Jerusalem will begin.

There are five prophetic events that will prepare the bride of Christ for the Day of the Lord, or the seventieth week, that is the last seven years of the church age what is referred to as the "Great Tribulation Period." Note: These five prophetic events were gleaned from a series of teachings by the Prophet Mike Bickles.

First, God is raising up prophets to the nation who will sound the alarm to the body of Christ. *"Blow ye the trumpet in Zion, and sound an alarm in my holy mountain: let all the inhabitants of the land tremble: for the day of the LORD cometh, for it is nigh at hand."* Joel 2:1. Thus, the tribulation period on the Day of the Lord will be "….a day of darkness and of gloominess." The prophet goes on to declare, "…the Day of the Lord is great and very terrible, and who can abide in it." The answer is simple, a people who will turn to God with all their heart, mind and soul: *"Therefore also now, saith the LORD, turn ye even to me with all your heart, and with fasting, and with weeping, and with mourning."* Joel 2:12.

The second prophetic event before the great tribulation period, as I see it, is the destruction of Russia as a world power. *"But I will remove far off from you the northern army, and will drive him into a land barren and desolate, with his face toward the east sea, and his hinder part toward the utmost sea, and his stink shall come up, and his ill savour shall come up, because he hath done great things."* Joel 2:20.

The third prophetic event as we approach the Day of the Lord is the revival and restoration of the church. In the midst of judgments and calamities, God Himself is going to restore His church to her original pattern of purity and power. *"Be glad then, ye children of Zion, and rejoice in the LORD your God: for he hath given you the former rain moderately,* *and he will cause to come down for you the rain, the former rain, and the latter rain in the first month."* Joel 2:23. The first church had the former rain, the last church will have the former rain and the latter rain. We are Haggai's last church. *"The glory of this latter house shall be greater than of the former, saith the LORD of hosts: and in this place will I give peace, saith the LORD of hosts."* Haggai 2:9.

The fourth prophetic event will be an outpouring of the Holy Spirit as we approach the Great Tribulation Period. *"And it shall come to pass afterward, that I will pour out my spirit upon all flesh; and your sons and your daughters shall prophesy, your old men shall dream dreams, your young men shall see visions: And also upon the servants and upon the handmaids in those days will I pour out my spirit. And I will shew wonders in the heavens and in the earth, blood, and fire, and pillars of smoke."* Joel 2:28-30. Again, as the church is restored in her authority, God will begin to pour out the Holy Spirit world-wide, and the gospel will be preached to every people group as a witness. So be it!

The fifth prophetic event into which we are moving is the rise of a one-world government. There are two signs that this Anti-Christ world government is forming. First, is the world-wide shaking of governments and the wars of the Middle East. *"And there shall be signs in the sun, and in the moon, and in the stars; and upon the earth distress of nations, with perplexity; the sea and the waves roaring."* Luke 21:25. The word "perplexity" means that the political leaders are unable to discover a way out of global effecting wars. The wars seem to be without end. There becomes a universal cry for peace. In the last seven centuries, Russia has been at war seventy percent of the time; Great Britain and France have been at war fifty-percent of the time. There are now 2.4 major wars breaking out each year. We are in the beginnings of Anti-Christ rebellion and world-wide confusion. We are being conditioned for a world government solution to birth a world peace movement.

Einstein said, "The secret of the bomb should be committed to a world government; either we find a way to establish a world government or we shall perish in the war of the atom." Nation after nation is developing the destructive atom bomb: Iran, North Korea, China, Pakistan, and India, to name a few! What world leader can offer solutions to this possible atomic holocaust?

There is also a world-wide cry for a solution in the Middle East, for someone or some group of leaders to settle the land dispute between the Jews and the Arab world. The word of God through Zechariah is happening or being fulfilled in our generation. *"Behold, I will make Jerusalem a cup of trembling unto all the people round about, when they shall be in the siege both against Judah and against Jerusalem."* Zechariah 12:2. The prophet Daniel said that there is a man coming who will settle this ancient dispute *"... He is the Anti-Christ he will come and ...He will make a covenant with Israel for one week."* Daniel 9:27. He will seemingly settle the Arab and Jewish dispute. But in the midst of the covenant, after three and a half years during this seven-year period, he will break covenant with Israel, overrun her and set up His Anti-Christ Kingdom.

The second prophetic sign of the forming of a world government is economic conditioning. *"And I stood upon the sand of the sea, and saw a beast rise up out of the sea, having seven heads and ten horns, and upon his horns ten crowns, and upon his heads the name of blasphemy."* Revelation 13:1. The sea is humanity, the beast is Anti-Christ, the ten horns are ten kings which could be the major ten nations of the European Common Market. The Anti-Christ will come into full world-wide influence through the economic system which I believe is being set-up through the Central Bankers. It seems that there are major economic power brokers who actually control most of the resources of our world economic system: oil and gas, gold and silver, to name a few. It is said by some, that these power brokers control the price of oil and even gasoline at the pumps. They dictate the volume of silver and gold on the market. I believe there is some truth to this theory. As Anti-Christ comes into control through the economic system…he will claim to be the Messiah; he will be worshipped and will attempt to set-up his kingdom in Jerusalem.

We are now in the first stages of economic control. The computer is already set-up in Belgium and every name of every person in the world is on it. Your name is on the Anti-Christ system now. We are moving toward a cashless society. I heard a testimony of a computer expert to whom Satan had spoken and told him that he might be the Anti-Christ if he kept moving in power. His mother, a spirit filled Christian, prayed for him and he was saved. However, he continued as an executive computer engineer and was involved in setting up the computer systems in Belgium. He felt compelled to quit knowing he was involved in setting up world economic control. When he prayed about it, God told him to continue because it had to be finished – it must be fulfilled to bring His word to pass. God is in control, and the Anti-Christ is in check. II Thessalonians 2:1 talks about the coming of the Lord Jesus Christ and the fulfillment of the Day of the Lord. In verses 2-7, *"Let no man deceive you by any means, for that day shall not come, except there come a falling away first, and that man of sin be revealed, the son of perdition;... For the mystery of iniquity doth already work; only he who now letteth will let, until he be taken out of the way. And then shall that wicked be revealed..."* He shall not be revealed, or come into full power until the restrainer is taken out of the world, and that is the Holy Spirit. He is the One who is restraining, checking, keeping the Anti-Christ from coming into full power until God's appointed time. The Anti-Christ cannot be revealed until the church is taken out, which seems to be scheduled to happen at mid-tribulation. The completion of God's wrath is in the last three and a half years of the seventieth week, when the Anti-Christ reveals himself and sets himself up in Jerusalem.

The "Day of the Lord" as described in the book of Revelation Chapter 6:1-7 and Chapter 8:1-2, the Lamb of God is worthy to open the seven-sealed book that will begin to release God's judgments against the Anti-Christ, and the nations that follow and worship Him. God's battle plan to cleanse the earth and usher in His Kingdom of righteousness begins. In the first seal, see the Anti-Christ and the nations that follow and worship Him, as God's battle plan to cleanse the earth and usher in His Kingdom of righteousness begins. In the first seal, Anti-Christ is introduced as he begins his reign of terror. As the Lamb opens the second, third, and fourth seals, God begins to break the staff of bread (world-wide food collapse) and releases the great sword judgments (one war begins to follow another). We are in the season of a world-wide collapse of the economy and escalating wars throughout planet earth. As the King of Kings opens the fifth seal, we see world-wide persecution of the church. Anti-Christ forces begin to kill those who are unashamed of Jesus as multitudes are being saved and believers begin to stand boldly against unrighteous governments. In the sixth seal, great earth quakes begin to occur. We are in the season of increasing earth quakes.

The rapture or translation of the church, which is the first resurrection, seems to occur before the final judgments of God against Anti-Christ and the rebellious nations who refused to repent. At this point at mid-tribulation, we may be seeing the fulfillment of Matthew 24:29-31 and I Thessalonians 4:13-17: *"Immediately after the tribulation of those days shall the sun be darkened, and the moon shall not give her light, and the stars shall fall from heaven, and the powers of the heavens shall be shaken: And then shall appear the sign of the Son of man in heaven: and then shall all the tribes of the earth mourn, and they shall see the Son of man coming in the clouds of heaven with power and great glory. And he shall send his angels with a great sound of a trumpet, and they shall gather together his elect from the four winds, from one end of heaven to the other."* Matthew 24:29-31. (Read I Thessalonians 4:13-17.) In both passages that describe the first resurrection, there is the sound of a trumpet. The trumpet follows the tribulation of those days in which God's judgments in the earth are in full manifestation against evil. In the sequence of the "Day of the Lord," God raises up the two witnesses who preach with great power and release God's final judgment on the Anti-Christ world system which will conclude the final three and a half years of the Great Tribulation Period. *"Immediately after the tribulation of those days shall the sun be darkened, and the moon shall not give her light, and the stars shall fall from heaven, and the powers of the heavens shall be shaken..."* Matthew 24:29.

    The third and final outpourings of judgments to eradicate evil are called the seven bowls of wrath. As I meditated upon these judgments, I recalled a promise, *"Much more then, being now justified by his blood, we shall be saved from wrath through him."* Romans 5:9. It's apparent that the body of Christ is not present during this final outpouring of God's wrath on a totally rebellious world system. The seven bowls of wrath are recorded in Revelation 16:1-21. Listed is a brief description of the same.

First bowl (sores): Painful sores on those who worship the Anti-Christ. (Revelation 16:1-2.)

Second bowl (food supply): Destroying the sea with blood and killing all in it. (Revelation 16:3.)

Third bowl (water supply): Poisoning the earth's fresh water with blood. (Revelation 16:4-7.)

Fourth bowl (torment): Scorching heat and fire from the sun. (Revelation 16:8-9.)

Fifth bowl (destruction): Darkness on the Anti-Christ's global empire. (Revelation 16:10-11.)

Sixth bowl (global guilt): Deceiving the nations to come to Armageddon. (Revelation 16:12-16.)

Seventh bowl (annihilation): Shaking by earthquakes and hail stones. (Revelation 16:17-21.) Mike Bickles, IHOP.

As the bowls of wrath are completed, the following is a three-fold sequence that ends the earth age:

1. **The final battle against the Anti-Christ system.** (The Battle of Armageddon.) *"And I saw heaven opened, and behold a white horse; and he that sat upon him was called Faithful and True, and in righteousness he doth judge and make war. His eyes were as a flame of fire, and on his head were many crowns; and he had a name written, that no man knew, but he himself. And he was clothed with a vesture dipped in blood: and his name is called The Word of God. And*

the armies which were in heaven followed him upon white horses, clothed in fine linen, white and clean. And out of his mouth goeth a sharp sword, that with it he should smite the nations: and he shall rule them with a rod of iron: and he treadeth the winepress of the fierceness and wrath of Almighty God. And he hath on his vesture and on his thigh a name written, KING OF KINGS, AND LORD OF LORDS. And I saw an angel standing in the sun; and he cried with a loud voice, saying to all the fowls that fly in the midst of heaven, Come and gather yourselves together unto the supper of the great God; That ye may eat the flesh of kings, and the flesh of captains, and the flesh of mighty men, and the flesh of horses, and of them that sit on them, and the flesh of all men, both free and bond, both small and great. And I saw the beast, and the kings of the earth, and their armies, gathered together to make war against him that sat on the horse, and against his army. And the beast was taken, and with him the false prophet that wrought miracles before him, with which he deceived them that had received the mark of the beast, and them that worshipped his image. These both were cast alive into a lake of fire burning with brimstone. And the remnant were slain with the sword of him that sat upon the horse, which sword proceeded out of his mouth: and all the fowls were filled with their flesh."* Revelation 19:11-21.

    2. **The binding of the serpent**. *"And I saw an angel come down from heaven, having the key of the bottomless pit and a great chain in his hand. And he laid hold on the dragon, that old serpent, which is the Devil, and Satan, and

bound him a thousand years, And cast him into the bottomless pit, and shut him up, and set a seal upon him, that he should deceive the nations no more, till the thousand years should be fulfilled: and after that he must be loosed a little season." Revelation 20:1-3.

3. **The souls of the first resurrection reign with Jesus as the Lord of Lords and the King of Kings for one thousand years on planet earth**. *"And I saw thrones, and they sat upon them, and judgment was given unto them: and I saw the souls of them that were beheaded for the witness of Jesus, and for the word of God, and which had not worshipped the beast, neither his image, neither had received his mark upon their foreheads, or in their hands; and they lived and reigned with Christ a thousand years. But the rest of the dead lived not again until the thousand years were finished. This is the first resurrection. Blessed and holy is he that hath part in the first resurrection: on such the second death hath no power, but they shall be priests of God and of Christ, and shall reign with him a thousand years"*. Revelation 20:4-6.

Let us rejoice as we see our redemption drawing near. Let's become part of a united prayer movement that will usher in God's final judgments, final outpourings and the final harvest of *"a great multitude which no man can number of all nations and kindreds, and people and tongues."* Revelation 7:9.

CHAPTER ELEVEN

God's Last Call For Intercessors

Throughout time and history, the Holy Spirit has always birthed a prayer movement to usher in the redemptive purposes of God. Often, He has called for prayer and fasting to stay His judgments in regards to the evil of a nation. II Chronicles 7:13:15 has always been a reference promise to release God's mercy on an undeserving people. First, that is a reference to God's judgments, *"If I shut up heaven that there be no rain, or if I command the locusts to devour the land, or if I send pestilence among my people."* II Chronicles 7:13. Then the Holy Spirit gives hope to His remnant with a conditional promise, *"If my people, which are called by my name, shall humble themselves, and pray, and seek my face, and turn from their wicked ways; then will I hear from heaven, and will forgive their sin, and will heal their land."* II Chronicles 7:14. The condition for staying His justified judgments is a core of godly people repenting and crying out for God's mercy and forgiveness. As He forgives the apathy and selfishness of His people He heals or restores their land.

The Lord began to reveal to His prophet Habakkuk the invasion of the land of Judah by the Chaldeans. In the first chapter of Habakkuk, the prophet complains to God about the abuse of justice among the Israelites. He states that, *"justice does not go forth as it should."* Habakkuk 1:4. No justice for the criminals *"...wrong justice proceeds..."* The righteous are being condemned and the wicked are justified; therefore, there is *"...spoiling and violence all around him..."* Habakkuk 1:3. In other words, there is a spirit of lawlessness in the land. Therefore, God Himself will punish the abuse of power by the sword judgment of war in which the armies of Chaldeans would bring desolation to the land of Judah. The redemptive judgments of God are the answer when a nation rebels and becomes violent with a spirit of lawlessness. This condition describes the state of our nation, the United States.

Again, in time and history, we see God's remedy to stay His judgments in regards to a nation: *"A prayer of Habakkuk the prophet upon Shigionoth. O LORD, I have heard thy speech, and was afraid: O LORD, revive thy work in the midst of the years, in the midst of the years make known; in wrath remember mercy."* Habakkuk 3:1-2. When the prophet heard the Lord's declaration of the Great Sword Judgment, the prophet feared and cried out for revival and mercy. And God responded to the heart cry of repentance and plea for mercy, *"God came from Teman...His glory covered the Heavens and the earth was full of His praise..."* Habakkuk 3:3. Revival is God coming in awesome power and irresistible holiness. Revival is God coming with His brilliance as His light dispels the darkness and cleanses the land of evil and injustice. My prayer for America: "Father God in wrath remember mercy… Father, we repent for the apathy of the body of Christ and for the rebellious sins of our nation…Father God, come, and fill our land with your glory!"

I am going to give one more Old Testament example of God using fervent prayer and fasting to stay His desolating judgments against an evil nation. The Lord sent Jonah to warn Nineveh which was an exceeding great city. *"…Jonah cried out and said, yet forty days and Nineveh shall be over thrown."* Jonah 3:4. The people of Nineveh took heed to the prophets warning and repented for their sins. Read this report of united prayer and fasting, *"So the people of Nineveh believed God, and proclaimed a fast, and put on sackcloth, from the greatest of them even to the least of them."* Jonah 3:5.

In response to prayer and fasting coupled with heart repentance, God stayed His judgments: *"And God saw their works, that they turned from their evil way; and God repented of the evil, that he had said that he would do unto them; and he did it not."* Jonah 3:10. This historic event took place somewhere between 760 and 746 B.C. Later in 620 B.C., the prophet Nahum predicted the destruction of Nineveh. (Read Nahum 2:1-13.) In May of 612 B.C., the Medes and the Babylonians laid siege to the Assyrian capital of Nineveh. The siege lasted for three months. In July of 612 B.C., the city fell. The fall of this great city shocked the ancient world. My purpose of stating the final outcome of Nineveh is that judgments can be stayed for a season, but not necessarily prevented. There is a plumbline that God stretches across a nation. *"Thus he shewed me: and, behold, the LORD stood upon a wall made by a plumbline, with a plumbline in his hand. And the LORD said unto me, Amos, what seest thou? And I said, A plumbline. Then said the LORD, Behold, I will set a plumbline in the midst of my people Israel: I will not again pass by them anymore."* Amos 7:7-8. I believe the Lord set a plumbline in the midst of our nation, and in 1973 we crossed it as we began to murder the unborn. Over this national sin, the judgments can be temporarily stayed by a unified repenting Body. But eventually, there will be justice for the unborn…God will bring justice through righteous punishment.

God's Justice in Regards to a Nation.

I have already written that God must judge a nation in this life or the earth age. In eternity, as individuals, we will face His judgments either at the judgment seat of Christ or the Great White Throne Judgment. However, the scales of a nation must be balanced in this life. Since, you and I are part of a nation; we must see and understand God's dealings in our land. Even now, America in under His increasing judgments. How, should the body of Christ, respond?

Simple, we respond as they did in history – through prayer and fasting. God is looking for a remnant, for a core of fervent intercessors who will stay His judgments and usher in His power. The Lord makes this call to and through the prophet, *"And I sought for a man among them, that should make up the hedge, and stand in the gap before me for the land, that I should not destroy it: but I found none."* Ezekiel 22:30. The Lord God was looking for someone who had a burden for their land and for the glory of God. Isaiah saw the kind of intercessors that the King of Glory was searching for to flow through.

The Salt of the Earth.

Jesus said, "Yea are the salt of the earth..." He expects us to manifest His presence on the earth to hinder the corruption of lawlessness which is the spirit of Anti-Christ. Derek Prince summed it up well, "As the salt of the earth, we who are Christ's disciples have two primary responsibilities. First, your presence we commend the earth to God's continuing grace and mercy. Second, by the power of the Holy Spirit within us, we hold in check the forces of corruption and lawlessness until God's appointed time." *Shaping History through Prayer and Fasting* by Derek Prince.

During the late 1970's, the Holy Spirit began to speak to me and burden for the plight of the unborn babies, over a million being murdered each year in the wombs of would-be mothers. This burden birthed a united prayer movement in the church where I was the senior pastor, Reserve Christian Church in Reserve, Louisiana. As a body, we would set apart days of prayer and fasting in repentance for this national sin. On one particular Saturday of prayer and fasting, the Holy Spirit prophetically spoke to us as a group, "My bow is bent and the arrow of judgment is pointed toward America.

Abortion must stop and you must stop it."

That word sent us to the streets of New Orleans, and we began to be the salt of the earth through an active presence at the abortion mills. Over the years, the salt has done her work. Hundreds, possibly thousands of unborn babies have been rescued from the knife of an abortionist. Several abortion clinics in New Orleans and Baton Rouge have been closed due to a manifested presence of God through His people – the salt. It amazed me to see the power of united prayer and fasting to express or declare the burden of the Lord. As we prayed and fasted, we became the answer to our own prayers. Our prayers put on feet that brought us in front of the murder mills to express the displeasure of our Father in heaven. The salt of the earth had its effect in partially stopping the corruption of abortions.

As Kings and Priests, We Rule Through Prayer.

As believers, we are in a place of authority and dominion. *"John to the seven churches which are in Asia: Grace be unto you, and peace, from him which is, and which was, and which is to come; and from the seven Spirits which are before his throne; And from Jesus Christ, who is the faithful witness, and the first begotten of the dead, and the prince of the kings of the earth. Unto him that loved us, and washed us from our sins in his own blood. And hath made us kings and priests unto God and his Father; to him be glory and dominion forever and ever. Amen."* Revelation 1:4-6. We are Kings and Priests unto the Lord. The resurrected Christ has been given us all authority and has delegated it to the apostolic church, that is, God's people who are under apostolic Fathers and prophets. We co-rule with Christ Jesus.

He has made us alive. We are in His resurrection, and we are enthroned with Him. Glory to God! Therefore, we share His kingly authority and eternal priesthood.

"The church is Christ's Body, in which He speaks and acts, by which He fills everything with His presence." Ephesians 1:23. The Father has appointed Jesus as supreme head of the church and supreme authority over every government and every dominion. The scripture declares that we share this authority with Him. As kings under Him, we have authority as His priests to decree His will through personal and united prayer. We have the authority and the power to carry out every good purpose of God on planet earth. The rise and fall of nations are won in the heavenlies through fervent intercessory power and the working of angelic powers.

We Have the Keys of the Kingdom.

Simon Peter confessed that Jesus is the Christ, meaning, God's anointed one to establish God's rule on planet earth. Jesus said that on this confession or revelation, I will build my church and the gates of hell will not prevail against her. Then, our Lord gave us the keys of the kingdom, that is, all authority in heaven and in earth. *"And I will give unto thee the keys of the kingdom of heaven: and whatsoever thou shalt bind on earth shall be bound in heaven: and whatsoever thou shalt loose on earth shall be loosed in heaven."* Matthew 16:19.

The keys are two-fold in application:

1. **As priests**, we see God's will and His purposes.

2. **As Kings**, we decree or release God's prayer through personal or united prayer.

As a biblical example, King Jehoshaphat humbled himself in prayer and fasting, to rescue his nation from the great sword judgment. (Read II Chronicles 20:1-30.) King Jehoshaphat turned to God for help, *"...Jehoshaphat proclaimed a fast throughout all Judea."* II Chronicles 20:3. In the humility of prayer and fasting, King Jehoshaphat cried out in utter dependence upon the delivering power of God. *"O our God, wilt thou not judge them? For we have no might against this great company that cometh against us; neither know we what to do: but our eyes are upon thee."* II Chronicles 20:12. In child-like dependency and surrender, the Holy Spirit responded, *"The spirit of the Lord came upon Zahaziel...And he said, Hearken ye, all Judah, and ye habitants of Jerusalem, and thou king Jehoshaphat, Thus saith the LORD unto you, Be not afraid nor dismayed by reason of this great multitude; for the battle is not yours, but God's."* II Chronicles 20:14-15. May this biblical account teach us what we must do for the deliverance of our nation. First, realize that we are surrounded by major principalities that have come to destroy our land. The principality of Islam threatens war and take-over. The principality of Humanism corrupts our media and every level of education. The principality of Socialism rules our federal government and threatens to take away our basic freedoms.

Secondly, the spiritual leaders of the body of Christ have a responsibility to humble ourselves and set our eyes on Almighty God for deliverance of our nation. As we do so, the Lord Himself will intervene and begin to turn the tables on the darkness that threatens to destroy the foundations of righteousness, justice and freedom.

Another example of intercessory prayer, using the keys of the kingdom, to stay God's judgments and rescue a nation, *"And it came to pass on the morrow, that Moses said unto the people, Ye have sinned a great sin: and now I will go up unto the LORD; peradventure I shall make an atonement for your sin."* Exodus 32:30. What was "the great sin" of Israel? Exodus 32:31 tells us, God's people lost their consciousness and commitment to the Lord their God. There was no fear of the Lord in their hearts. They were in the sin of idolatry which has root in covetousness. (Read Ephesians 5:5.) Covetousness means to place temporal values before values; to seek first the material world rather than seek first the Kingdom of God and His righteousness.

Moses was a fervent intercessor: *"And it came to pass, as soon as he came nigh unto the camp, that he saw the calf, and the dancing: and Moses' anger waxed hot, and he cast the tables out of his hands, and brake them beneath the mount."* Exodus 32:19. Five reasons why Moses' heart waxed hot which resulted in fervent intercession:

1. **Moses had seen the holiness of God**. He had been in the presence of God and could see the idolatry of God's

people. The more we are in His presence, the hotter our heart will burn for His will and the exoneration of His name.

2. **They had forsaken God.** They rebelled against a merciful Father who had delivered them from the tyranny of Pharaoh. They had forsaken the fountain of living water to satisfy the lust of their flesh and the lust of their hearts. *"And the LORD said unto Moses, Go, get thee down; for thy people, which thou broughtest out of the land of Egypt, have corrupted themselves."* Exodus 32:7.

3. **He had to wear a veil because the brightness of the light exuded off of him. He was full of God's light and salt.** He could not stand the sight of sin nor could sin stand the sight of him. In the fullness of the Lord's presence, he had a fervent zeal for the Father's heart and His will for God's people. James declares that the effectual fervent prayer of a believer has much prayer because of a burden for God's name and His righteousness. (Read James 5:6.)

4. **The effectual fervent prayer of a righteous people must believe that God has a plan and hope for their nation.** (Read Exodus 32:9-12.) God was prepared to destroy the nation of Israel but Moses reminded God of His mighty deliverance and plan for their freedom. Does God still have a plan for America or is America beyond recovery to be restored to a state of righteousness and goodness? As long as God has a salty remnant of prayer warriors and activists, there is hope.

5. Moses fervent prayer was based on covenant promises. *"Remember Abraham, Isaac, and Israel, thy servants, to whom thou swarest by thine own self, and saidst unto them, I will multiply your seed as the stars of heaven, and all this land that I have spoken of will I give unto your seed, and they shall inherit it forever. And the LORD repented of the evil which he thought to do unto his people."* Exodus 32:13-14. A covenant is a transaction between God and man. It is a contract agreement which results in divine union. It is a fusion where we become God-men. In covenant, God is the senior partner and we are the junior partner. He offers a covenant of redemption with provision, protection, blessings, and responsibilities.

God's covenant has a four-fold purpose:

1. It is the basis of revelation for God to reveal Himself to man. The Holy Spirit works within the promises and commands of covenant or within the agreement between God and man.

2. Secondly, covenant gives government the moral and civil law which brings unity and peace to a people. This is the basis of our constitution and forms the basic structure of the local church.

3. Thirdly, the contract agreement dictates areas of responsibility and obedience. *"And he took the book of the covenant, and read in the audience of the people: and they said, All that the LORD hath said will we do, and be*

obedient." Exodus 24:7.

4. Finally, the covenant spells out our inheritance, our rights, our promises and privileges. Indeed, the Bible is our book of covenant promises.

When we are in covenant, we come into divine union with our heavenly Father. In divine union, we take on the name of the Lord. *"Neither shall thy name any more be called Abram, but thy name shall be Abraham; for a father of many nations have I made thee."* Genesis 17:5. God's old covenant name was Yahweh. In His name, the H is the prominent letter. In Abram, God added H to his name; he took on the name of God, "The Father of Nations!" In a marriage covenant, a woman takes on the name of her husband; that is, he becomes her headship and authority; her protector and provider.

Four things happen in the marriage covenant:

1. She gets his love and leadership.

2. She gets his protection and provision.

3. She gets his duties and babies.

4. She gets his name. She becomes the name bearer of the covenant contract. Therefore, she gets the power of attorney of his name. In covenant, she has the right to use his name to write checks and do other business transactions.

In a covenant with God, believers become name bearers. The disciples were first called Christians at Antioch.

We have become the name bearers of our Lord. We are his representation on earth. We have been called to reveal Him to man, to fulfill His purposes on earth in that no one should perish but that everyone would come to repentance. We have His provision, protection, love and leadership, responsibilities and duties, and the power of His name. Listen to these two exceedingly great promises of our covenant: *"And whatsoever ye shall ask in my name, that will I do, that the Father may be glorified in the Son."* John 14:13. *"If my people, which are called by my name, shall humble themselves, and pray, and seek my face, and turn from their wicked ways; then will I hear from heaven, and will forgive their sin, and will heal their land."* II Chronicles 7:14.

We have the power of attorney of His name. We co-rule with Him! We have all authority in heaven and in earth! Let us see His heart. Let us use His name. Let us take back our nation. Let us go into every nation and preach the gospel. Let us be the last church full of His presence and power. Let us push back the darkness and usher in the second coming of Christ.

Need additional copies?

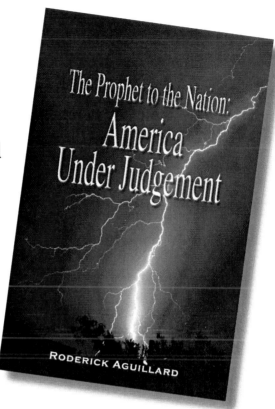

To order more copies of
The Prophet to the Nation:
America Under Judgement

contact NewBookPublishing.com

- ❐ Order online at NewBookPublishing.com
- ❐ Call 877-311-5100 or
- ❐ Email Info@NewBookPublishing.com

Call for multiple copy discounts!